EASA PRIVATE PILOT LICENCE
– AEROPLANE –
AIRCRAFT GENERAL

Before attempting these practice examination papers, you should have read Air Pilot's Manual, Volume 4 – The Aeroplane Technical and have completed the Progress Tests throughout the manual.

The Aircraft General examination consists of 16 questions; the time allowed is 35 minutes. Each of the practice examination papers that follow contain 20 questions.

The pass mark is 75%.

Please read each question carefully and ensure you understand it fully before making your choice of answer.

Each question is multiple choice with four possible answers A, B, C and D. You should indicate your chosen answer by placing a cross in the appropriate box on the answer sheet.

Blank answer sheets are to be found at the end of this publication, these may be photocopied.

INTENTIONALLY BLANK

TO ACCOMPANY

AIR PILOT'S MANUAL - VOLUME 4

Questions, Answers & Explanations

EASA PPL Revision Papers

Aircraft General

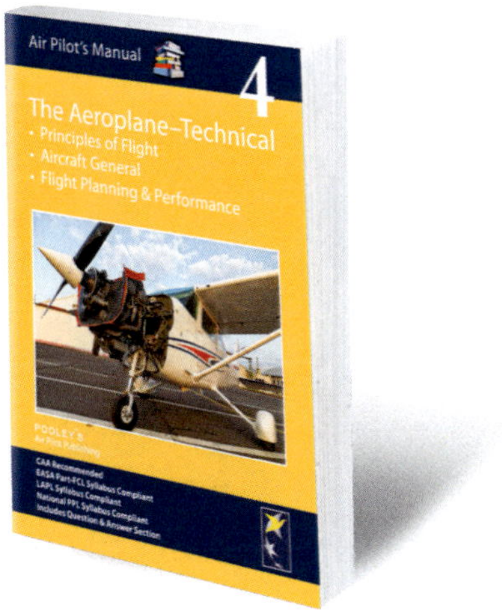

Written and illustrated by
Helena B A Hughes

POOLEYS
Air Pilot Publishing

EASA Private Pilot Licence Aeroplane Questions, Answers & Explanations – Aircraft General

ISBN 978-1-84336-206-7

First Edition published February 2014
Reprinted June 2014
Reprinted February 2016
Reprinted January 2017
Revised Edition July 2017

Origination by Pooleys Flight Equipment Limited.

Published by Pooleys Flight Equipment Ltd

Elstree Aerodrome
Hertfordshire WD6 3AW
Tel: +44(0)20 8953 4870
Web: www.pooleys.com
Email: sales@pooleys.com

AUTHOR

Helena B A Hughes

Helena Hughes was born into an aviation household, having her first informal "flying lesson" at the age of four. Her late father David was a flying instructor and also flew corporate jets. On leaving University Helena obtained her PPL. Shortly afterwards she started work in Air Traffic Control at London Luton Airport earning her Controllers Licence in 1990. Helena continues to be an operational Air Traffic Control Officer and is currently posted to Swanwick working "Thames Radar", "Luton Radar" and "Heathrow Special"; she is involved in controller training as both an Instructor and Assessor. Helena holds a fixed wing CPL/IR and has been a flying instructor since 1996. She also holds a PPL(H) and is a Radio Telephony and Air/Ground Examiner.

Helena would like to thank: Mrs. Brenda "Bedda" Hughes; Mr. Andrew Temple of Solent Flight Ltd; A Vrancken and H Ewing

INTRODUCTION

This book is intended as an aid to revision and examination preparation for those studying for the grant of an EASA PPL. Ideally its use should follow a period of self or directed study to consolidate the knowledge acquired and identify any areas of weakness prior to attempting the PPL examinations themselves.

The questions and answers in this publication are designed to reflect those appearing in the current examination papers and are set out in a representative format. No attempt has been made to replicate any actual examination paper.

Blank answer sheets are provided at the end of the book which may be photocopied to enable multiple attempts at each exam.

EDITORS

Dorothy Saul-Pooley LLB(Hons) FRAeS

Dorothy holds an ATPL (A) and a CPL (H), and is both an instructor and examiner on aeroplanes and an instructor on helicopters. She is Head of Training for a school dedicated to running Flight Instructor courses at Shoreham. She is also a CAA Flight Instructor Examiner. In addition, having qualified as a solicitor in 1982, Dorothy acted for many years as a consultant specialising in aviation and insurance liability issues, and has lectured widely on air law and insurance issues. This highly unusual combination of qualifications led to her appointment as Honorary Solicitor to the Guild of Air Pilots and Navigators (GAPAN). Dorothy is a Fellow of the Royal Aeronautical Society, first Chairman of the GAPAN Instructor Committee, and past Chairman of the Education & Training Committee. She has just completed her term of office as the Master for the year 2014-15 of the Honourable Company of Air Pilots (formerly GAPAN). She is also Chairman of the Professional Flying Instructors Association. In 2003 she was awarded the Jean Lennox Bird Trophy for her contribution to aviation and support of Women in Aviation and the BWPA (British Women Pilots Association). In 2013 Dorothy was awarded the prestigious Master Air Pilots Certificate by GAPAN. A regular contributor to seminars, conferences and aviation publications. Dorothy is the author and editor of a number of flying training books and has published articles in legal and insurance journals.

Daljeet Gill BA(Hons)

Daljeet is the Head of Design & Development for Pooleys Flight Equipment and editor of the Air Pilot's Manuals, Guides to the EASA IR & CPL Flight Test, Pre-flight Briefing and R/T Communications as well as many other publications. Daljeet has been involved with the editing, typesetting and designing of all Pooleys publications and products since she joined us in 2001. Graduating in 1999 with a BA(Hons) in Graphic Design, she deals with marketing, advertising, exhibition design and technical design of our manufactured products in the UK. She maintains our website and produces our Pooleys Catalogue. Daljeet's design skills and imaginative approach have brought a new level of clarity and readability to the projects she has touched.

Sebastian Pooley FRIN MRAeS

Sebastian is Managing Director of Pooleys Flight Equipment and a Director of Air Pilot Publishing. He holds a PPL (A). Sebastian is a Committee Member of the GANG - the General Aviation Navigation Group, part of the Royal Institute of Navigation and a judge for the International Dawn to Dusk Competition. He is a Liveryman of the Honourable Company of Air Pilots, a Fellow of the Royal Institute of Navigation and a Member of the Royal Aeronautical Society.

AIRCRAFT GENERAL PAPER 1

1. In a four-stroke piston engine a normal "Otto" cycle each valve will open:

   a. Twice
   b. Three times
   c. Once
   d. Four times

2. The compression ratio is:

   a. Cylinder volume when piston is TDC : Cylinder volume when piston is BDC
   b. Total cylinder volume : Volume when piston is BDC
   c. Cylinder volume when piston is BDC : Cylinder volume when piston is TDC
   d. Total cylinder volume : swept volume

3. During one complete "Otto" cycle each piston will move:

   a. Up once and down once
   b. Up twice and down once
   c. Up once and down twice
   d. Up twice and down twice

4. The cylinders of a piston engine are finned in order to:

   a. Decrease weight
   b. Improve cooling by increasing their surface area
   c. Increase the strength of the cylinder
   d. Streamline airflow around the cylinder

5. The cockpit oil temperature gauge is connected to a temperature probe. The probe senses the temperature of the oil:

   a. In the hottest part of the engine
   b. After it has passed the oil cooler, but before it is used within the hot sections of the engine
   c. Before the oil cooler
   d. In the oil sump

6. A "wet sump" lubrication system is one where:

   a. A scavenger pump collects oil from the sump and returns it to an oil tank
   b. Oil is not required for cooling and lubrication
   c. Oil is contained in a sump at the bottom of the engine and there is no oil tank
   d. An oil tank is used to re-fill the sump as necessary

7. Excessive oil pressure is prevented by:

   a. A pressure relief valve
   b. A non return valve
   c. A high capacity pressure pump
   d. A filter by-pass valve

8. In the event of an oil cooler blockage in flight, a by-pass valve will operate to circumvent the cooler. The by-pass valve is:

   a. Manually selected
   b. Temperature activated
   c. Density dependent
   d. Pressure dependent

9. The oil pressure gauge indicates the oil pressure at the:

a. Outlet side of the pressure pump
b. Inlet side of the pressure pump
c. Difference between the inlet side of the pressure pump and the outlet side
d. Difference between pressure at the pressure pump and pressure at the scavenger pump

10. A "dry sump" lubrication system is one where:

a. Oil is not required for cooling and lubrication
b. Oil is contained in a sump at the bottom of the engine and there is no oil tank
c. A scavenge pump collects oil from the sump and returns it to an oil tank
d. An oil tank is used to re-fill the sump as necessary

11. Some of the main uses of oil within an engine are:

a. Lubrication, heating and sealing
b. Lubrication, cleaning and heating
c. Lubrication, cooling and cleaning
d. Cooling, shock absorption and lubrication

12. When starting a cold engine, if the oil pressure gauge does not register a rise within around 30 seconds you should:

a. Leave the RPM at idle to allow the engine to warm up and the oil pressure to rise
b. Stop the engine immediately to avoid damage
c. Increase the RPM to try to increase the oil pressure
d. Ignore it, the low oil temperature is probably the cause, sufficient oil was observed during the visual inspection

13. During flight you notice that the oil pressure is fluctuating and indicating lower than normal together with a rise in the oil temperature. You should:

a. Monitor the readings, but continue as planned. Gauges are notoriously unreliable
b. Reduce power to improve cooling
c. Enrichen the mixture and apply power to increase the pressure
d. Land as soon as possible

14. A cowling fitted to an air-cooled aircraft engine is to:

a. Form a protective envelope around the engine and to retain heat
b. Duct air around the cylinders to heat them evenly and to reduce drag
c. Duct air around the cylinders to cool them evenly and to increase drag
d. Duct air around the cylinders to cool them evenly and to reduce drag

15. Prior to start, when priming the engine the fuel is usually delivered into:

a. The carburettor
b. The cylinder combustion chamber
c. The inlet valve port or the induction manifold
d. The fuel booster pump

16. It is essential that the correct grade of fuel is used. Avgas or 100LL is coloured ...(i)... all labels relating to this fuel are coloured ...(ii)...

a. i) blue ii) red
b. i) red ii) blue
c. i) blue ii) black
d. i) yellow ii) red

17. If water is present in the fuel system it will cause:

a. Icing
b. Contamination and loss of engine power
c. The fuel to freeze
d. Carburettor icing

18. By weight the ideal fuel: air ratio is roughly:

a. 1:1
b. 1:8
c. 1:12
d. 1:21

19. The white arc on the airspeed indicator shows the:

a. Caution range
b. Normal operating range
c. Flap operating range
d. V_{NE} range

20. One possible cause of "nose wheel shimmy" is:

a. Incorrect tyre pressures
b. Incorrect oleo pressures
c. Excessive tyre creep
d. The failure of the torque link

END OF AIRCRAFT GENERAL PAPER 1

AIRCRAFT GENERAL
PAPER 1: ANSWERS

No	A	B	C	D
1			X	
2			X	
3				X
4		X		
5		X		
6			X	
7	X			
8				X
9	X			
10			X	
11			X	
12		X		
13				X
14				X
15			X	
16	X			
17		X		
18			X	
19			X	
20				X

CORRECT ANSWERS: PERCENTAGES					
15	16	17	18	19	20
75%	80%	85%	90%	95%	100%

1. **(Answer: C)** During an Otto cycle each valve will open once.

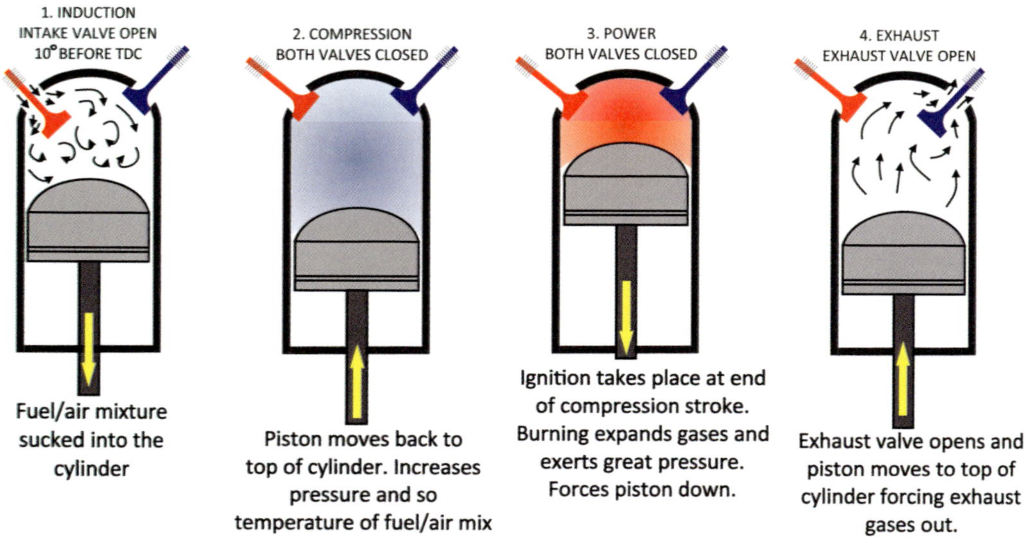

FURTHER READING: APM VOLUME 4, SECTION 2, CHAPTER 16 – THE AEROPLANE ENGINE

2. **(Answer: C)** Compression ratio is the ratio between the total cylinder volume (piston bottom dead centre) compared to the clearance volume (piston top dead centre). **Compression ratio = Total volume: Clearance volume**

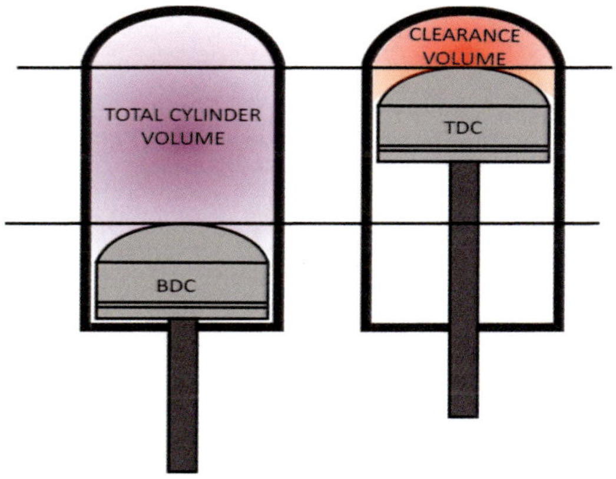

FURTHER READING: APM VOLUME 4, SECTION 2, CHAPTER 16 – THE AEROPLANE ENGINE

3. **(Answer: D)** During one Otto cycle the piston will move up twice and down twice.

FURTHER READING: APM VOLUME 4, SECTION 2, CHAPTER 16 – THE AEROPLANE ENGINE

4. **(Answer: B)** Cylinders are finned to improve cooling

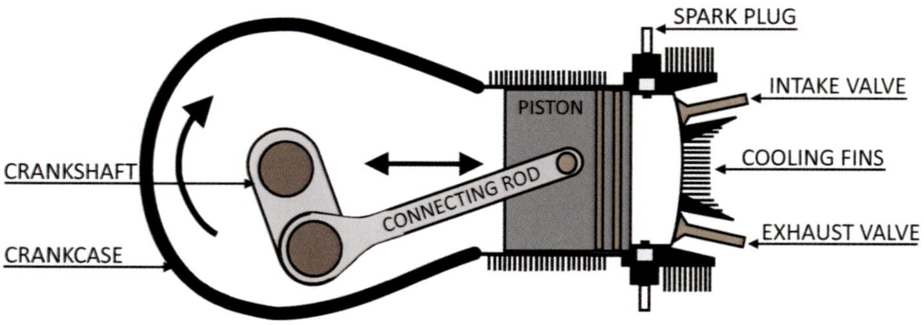

WET SUMP

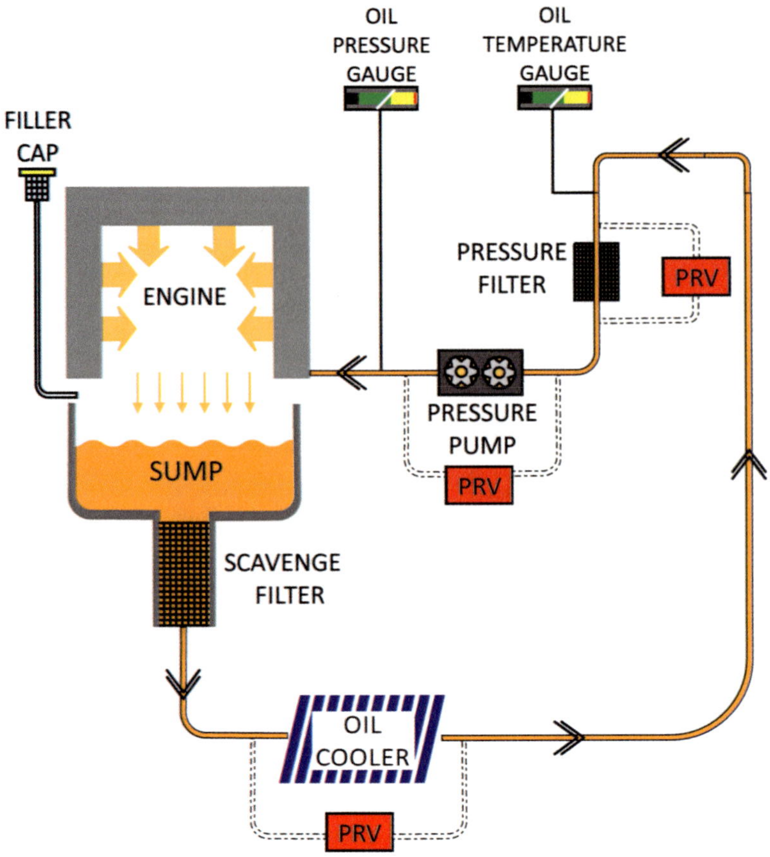

DRY SUMP

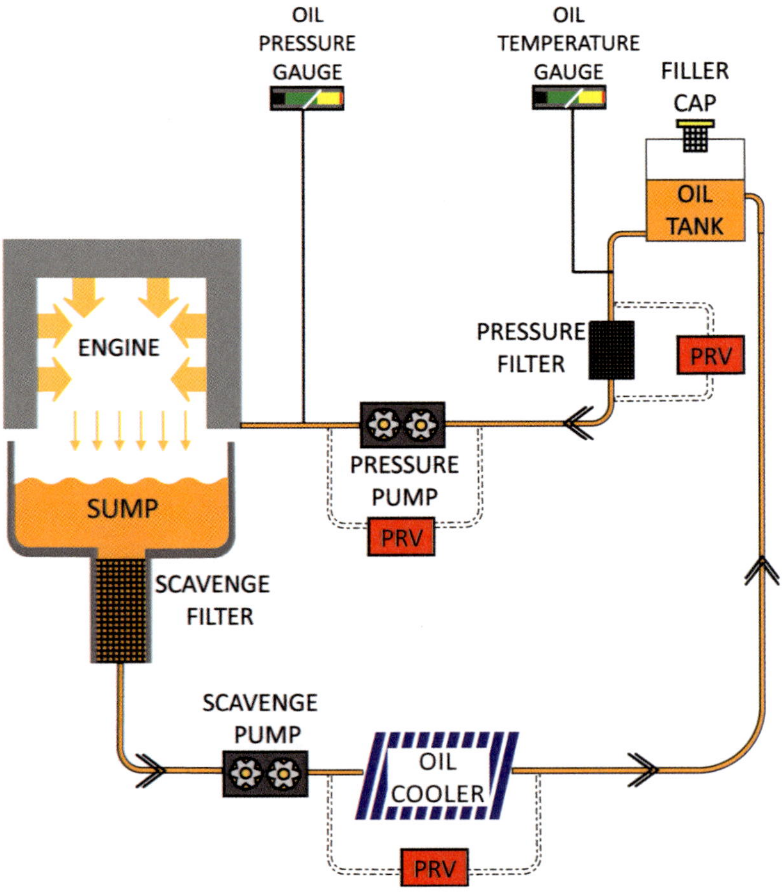

FURTHER READING: APM VOLUME 4, SECTION 2, CHAPTER 16 – THE AEROPLANE ENGINE

5. **(Answer: B)** The probe senses the temperature of the oil after it has passed the oil cooler, but before it is used within the hot sections of the engine.

FURTHER READING: APM VOLUME 4, SECTION 2, CHAPTER 19 – THE OIL SYSTEM

6. **(Answer: C)** A wet sump system does not have a storage tank, instead oil is collected at the bottom of the engine. A pressure pump will draw oil directly from the sump via a scavenger filter and a pressure filter from where it continues into the main oil gallery.

FURTHER READING: APM VOLUME 4, SECTION 2, CHAPTER 19 – THE OIL SYSTEM

7. **(Answer: A)** Excessive oil pressure is relieved by a pressure relief valve. This will be situated downstream of the pump, and when open the PRV will allow some oil to route back to the inlet side of the pressure pump.

FURTHER READING: APM VOLUME 4, SECTION 2, CHAPTER 19 – THE OIL SYSTEM

8. **(Answer: D)** A blockage in the oil cooler could be extremely serious leading to starvation of oil to the main gallery and failure of the engine. Should this occur a pressure relief valve will activate allowing oil to by-pass the cooler.

FURTHER READING: APM VOLUME 4, SECTION ?, CHAPTER 19 – THE OIL SYSTEM

9. **(Answer: A)** The reading on the oil pressure gauge is taken from the outlet side of the pressure pump.

FURTHER READING: APM VOLUME 4, SECTION 2, CHAPTER 19 – THE OIL SYSTEM

10. **(Answer: C)** A dry sump system scavenges oil from the bottom of the engine and returns it to an oil storage tank. The scavenge pump will have a larger capacity than the pressure pump to ensure the supply to the oil tank.

FURTHER READING: APM VOLUME 4, SECTION 2, CHAPTER 19 – THE OIL SYSTEM

11. **(Answer: C)** Some of the main uses for oil in an engine are:

- *Lubrication, allowing two metal surfaces to move past one another without actually touching.*
- *Cooling, to help dissipate any heat generated by friction and from combustion. The oil itself is cooled by having an oil cooler incorporated in the system.*
- *Cleaning, oil circulation around the engine will carry away dirt and any foreign particles. Any contaminants are removed by the oil filter.*

FURTHER READING: APM VOLUME 4, SECTION 2, CHAPTER 19 – THE OIL SYSTEM

12. **(Answer: B)** When starting a cold engine, if the oil pressure gauge does not register a rise within around 30 seconds you should stop the engine immediately to avoid damaging the engine. After an aircraft has been standing oil will drain from the oil galleries and collect in the sump, or at the bottom of the crankcase. One other factor to consider is that in cold weather the oil will become thicker and more viscous which will hinder its flow around the engine. On start 30 seconds will allow time for the oil to begin to circulate and, if the system is operating normally, for pressure to register.

FURTHER READING: APM VOLUME 4, SECTION 2, CHAPTER 19 – THE OIL SYSTEM

13. (Answer: D) Fluctuating oil pressure together with increasing oil temperature is associated with low oil quantity. Insufficient oil will cause a rise in oil temperature, as the lack of oil will not transport heat from the engine's hot areas nor lubricate effectively. Low quantity may also cause the pump to cavitate leading to pressure fluctuations. Cavitation is where vapour bubbles form in a flowing liquid due to low pressure. No oil = engine seizure = land as soon as possible.

FURTHER READING: APM VOLUME 4, SECTION 2, CHAPTER 19 – THE OIL SYSTEM

14. (Answer: D) Engine cowlings are installed to ensure correct operating temperatures are maintained by promoting even cooling. This is achieved by ducting air inside the cowling around the engine. The cowling also streamlines the airflow around the engine, reducing drag.

FURTHER READING: APM VOLUME 4, SECTION 2, CHAPTER 20 – THE COOLING SYSTEM

15. (Answer: C) To aid starting a cold engine a hand operated primer pump is used to inject fuel directly into the induction manifold near the combustion chamber or to the inlet valve port.

Cold air is also very dense meaning that fuel entering the chamber is reluctant to evaporate, priming adds extra fuel so that some will evaporate and sustain combustion. It is essential that the primer is locked after use and during flight. Leaving it open may lead to excessive fuel entering the cylinders meaning the fuel/air mixture will become too rich, which could stop the engine (a "rich cut").

FURTHER READING: APM VOLUME 4, SECTION 2, CHAPTER 18 – THE FUEL SYSTEM

16. (Answer: A) Grade 100LL fuel is dyed blue. All labels relating to the delivery and storage of 100LL are red.

FURTHER READING: APM VOLUME 4, SECTION 2, CHAPTER 18 – THE FUEL SYSTEM

17. (Answer: B) Water entering the engine will cause a loss of power, or worse, cause the engine to stop. This is why the contents of the fuel tanks are checked before each flight. Water has a higher specific gravity than Avgas and will therefore settle to the bottom of the fuel tanks and appear as a "bubble" at the bottom of the fuel tester tube.

FURTHER READING: APM VOLUME 4, SECTION 2, CHAPTER 18 – THE FUEL SYSTEM

18. (Answer: C) By weight the fuel: air ratio should be approximately 1 part fuel to 12 parts air. At altitude the weight of air is less, therefore the mixture should be leaned to maintain the ratio. If the mixture is too lean detonation could occur. If the mixture is too rich the engine will not run efficiently and less power will be generated.

FFURTHER READING: APM VOLUME 4, SECTION 2, CHAPTER 18 – THE FUEL SYSTEM

19. **(Answer: C)** The white arc on the airspeed indicator shows the flap operating range.

FURTHER READING: APM VOLUME 4, SECTION 3, CHAPTER 25 – PRESSURE INSTRUMENTS

20. **(Answer: D)** One possible cause of "nose wheel shimmy" is the failure of the torque link. Aircraft with oleo-pneumatic units are prone to nose wheel shimmy, where the nose wheel oscillates a few degrees either side of centre as it runs along the ground creating unpleasant and possibly damaging vibrations. Often, to prevent shimmy a "shimmy damper" is fitted to the nose wheel; shimmy could also result if this unit is under pressurised.

FURTHER READING: APM VOLUME 4, SECTION 2, CHAPTER 24 – LANDING GEAR, TYRES AND BRAKES

END OF EXPLANATIONS PAPER 1

INTENTIONALLY BLANK

AIRCRAFT GENERAL PAPER 2

1. With increase in altitude, air density will ...(i)... if not adjusted the fuel: air mixture will become ...(ii)...:

   a. i) increase ii) weaker
   b. i) increase ii) richer
   c. i) decrease ii) weaker
   d. i) decrease ii) richer

2. In a piston engine the idle cut-off valve:

   a. Increases fuel flow to the engine at idle power
   b. Cannot be operated when the engine is above idle power
   c. Stops fuel flow from the discharge nozzle
   d. Helps the engine to run at idle power settings

3. To achieve the best fuel: air mix when operating at altitude the mixture control is moved towards the lean position until engine RPM:

   a. Decreases, then the mixture control is moved slightly to the rich side of peak RPM
   b. Decreases, then the mixture control is moved slightly to the lean side of peak RPM
   c. Increases, then the control is moved slightly to the rich side of peak RPM
   d. Increases, then the control is moved slightly to the lean side of peak RPM

4. When operating at high power, over 75%, a richer mixture is desirable because:

   a. High power will lead to high pressure in the cylinders
   b. The air in the cylinders will be more dense
   c. Any excess fuel will be used to heat the engine
   d. Any excess fuel will be used to cool the engine

5. Aircraft types that are permitted to use MOGAS are promulgated in:

   a. Aeronautical Information Circulars
   b. CAA Airworthiness Notices
   c. NOTAMs
   d. ICAO document 1224

6. Baffles are fitted within the engine cowling to:

   a. Increase the strength of the cowling
   b. Direct the flow of air evenly around all cylinders to aid cooling
   c. Decrease the area for air leaving the engine compartment
   d. Control the volume of air entering the engine compartment

7. In a four-stoke piston engine the purpose of the crankshaft is to:

   a. Convert rotary motion into linear motion
   b. Convert reciprocating motion into rotary motion
   c. Control the inlet and exhaust valve recoil
   d. Convert rotary motion into reciprocating

8. In a four-stroke piston engine for every revolution of the crankshaft the camshaft will rotate:

   a. Once, it operates at engine speed
   b. Twice, the camshaft operates at twice engine speed
   c. Half a revolution, the camshaft operates at half engine speed
   d. Four times, it operates at twice engine speed

9. Air flow through the carburettor venturi creates a:

- **a.** Rise in pressure and an increase in velocity at the carburettor throat
- **b.** Rise in pressure and a decrease in velocity at the carburettor throat
- **c.** Drop in pressure and a decrease in velocity at the carburettor throat
- **d.** Drop in pressure and an increase in velocity at the carburettor throat

10. In a carburettor the purpose of an accelerator pump is to:

- **a.** Avoid a weak-cut when the throttle is rapidly advanced
- **b.** Increase fuel delivery pressure
- **c.** Ensure sufficient fuel is available at altitude
- **d.** Ensure the correct volume of fuel is delivered to the cylinders

11. In a simple carburettor the pressure in the float chamber compared to the pressure at the venturi is:

- **a.** The same
- **b.** Lower
- **c.** Higher
- **d.** Variable and dependent upon the RPM selected

12. The purpose of the idling jet is to:

- **a.** Prevent a weak cut when the throttle is opened quickly
- **b.** Keep the engine running at low RPM by providing fuel near the butterfly
- **c.** Prevent the main jet giving too much fuel at low RPM
- **d.** Keep the engine running at low RPM by providing fuel directly into the cylinders

13. You are flying over the UK, clear of precipitation with an air temperature of + 14°C and a relative humidity of 40%. Serious carburettor icing would be likely to occur when:

- **a.** Operating at full power
- **b.** Operating at cruise power
- **c.** Operating at any power setting
- **d.** Operating at descent power

14. On engine start, after releasing the starter button if the starter warning light stays on you should:

- **a.** Increase the engine RPM until the light goes out
- **b.** Monitor the light for exactly one minute, if it remains on at the end of that time stop the engine
- **c.** Check the alternator output level
- **d.** Stop the engine immediately to avoid damage to the engine and/or starter motor

15. In a piston engine the high tension supply to the spark plugs is derived from:

- **a.** The battery during start and the magneto once the engine is running
- **b.** The magneto's self contained generation and distribution system
- **c.** The battery
- **d.** The magneto during start and the battery once the engine is running

16. When a magneto is switched off, the switch in the primary circuit is:

- **a.** Closed and the primary circuit is earthed
- **b.** Closed and the primary circuit is not earthed
- **c.** Open and the primary circuit is not earthed
- **d.** Open and the primary circuit is earthed

17. When a magneto becomes detached from its ignition switch:

a. The engine will fail to stop when both magnetos are selected to "Off"
b. There is an instant drop in RPM
c. The engine will fail if the other magneto is switched off
d. The engine will run roughly

18. Under normal running conditions a magneto draws its primary circuit current from:

a. The battery
b. The generator
c. A ground power unit
d. Its self-contained electro-magnetic induction system

19. V_{NE} is the:

a. Stalling speed gear down, flaps lowered and power off
b. Stalling speed gear up, flaps up and power off
c. Maximum structural cruise speed
d. Never exceed speed

20. Load factors for an aircraft in the aerobatic category compared to one certified in the normal or utility category will be:

a. Lower
b. Higher than normal, but less than utility
c. Higher
d. Higher than utility, but less than normal

END OF AIRCRAFT GENERAL PAPER 2

AIRCRAFT GENERAL
PAPER 2: ANSWERS

No	A	B	C	D
1				X
2			X	
3	X			
4				X
5		X		
6		X		
7		X		
8			X	
9				X
10	X			
11			X	
12		X		
13				X
14				X
15		X		
16	X			
17	X			
18				X
19				X
20			X	

CORRECT ANSWERS: PERCENTAGES					
15	16	17	18	19	20
75%	80%	85%	90%	95%	100%

AIRCRAFT GENERAL PAPER 2: EXPLANATIONS

1. **(Answer: D)** With increase in altitude, air density reduces and if not adjusted the fuel: air mixture will become richer. An overly rich mixture will lead to the engine running roughly and if not corrected possibly a rich cut.

FURTHER READING: APM VOLUME 4, SECTION 2, CHAPTER 18 – THE FUEL SYSTEM

2. **(Answer: C)** The idle cut-off is the usual way of shutting down the engine in a light aircraft. When the mixture control is moved to the idle cut-off position, the ICO valve stops fuel flow from the discharge nozzle. Normally the engine will continue to run for a few seconds whilst all remaining fuel in the cylinders and inlet manifold is burned.

FURTHER READING: APM VOLUME 4, SECTION 2, CHAPTER 18 – THE FUEL SYSTEM

3. **(Answer: A)** To lean the mixture the mixture control should be moved slowly towards the lean position. As the correct fuel: air ratio is achieved the RPM will increase, but with further leaning the RPM will decrease and will be combined with a slight roughness in the running of the engine.

   From this point the mixture control should then be moved towards the rich position until the best RPM is achieved and the engine runs smoothly. The chemically correct mixture is now feeding the engine.

   Finally the mixture should be enrichened a little more, to ensure that the engine is running just on the rich side of the chemically correct mixture. Remember fuel also serves a cooling function.

FURTHER READING: APM VOLUME 4, SECTION 2, CHAPTER 18 – THE FUEL SYSTEM

4. **(Answer: D)** Fuel is also a cooling agent, if a rich mixture is selected excess fuel entering the combustion chamber will evaporate and absorb heat from the cylinder head. This will help to maintain an optimum operating temperature.

   Situations where this may be useful include climbing where low airspeed (and therefore less air cooling) combined with high power may lead to an increase in cylinder head temperature.

   Any power setting above 75% is deemed to be "high", in the cruise aircraft piston engines are generally operated between 60 to 65%.

FURTHER READING: APM VOLUME 4, SECTION 2, CHAPTER 18 – THE FUEL SYSTEM

5. **(Answer: B)** Aircraft types that are approved to use MOGAS are detailed in CAA Airworthiness Notices, specifically number 98. Generally the use of MOGAS is not permitted as the quality control systems that are in place for AVGAS are not present; also motor fuel is more volatile and evaporates more readily which could lead to vapour locks in an aircraft's fuel system and possibly fuel starvation. Other problems are that using MOGAS in light aircraft can lead to low power output, fouling of the spark plugs and detonation.

FURTHER READING: APM VOLUME 4, SECTION 2, CHAPTER 18 – THE FUEL SYSTEM

6. **(Answer: B)** Baffles are fitted to direct cooling air as evenly as possible around the cylinders.

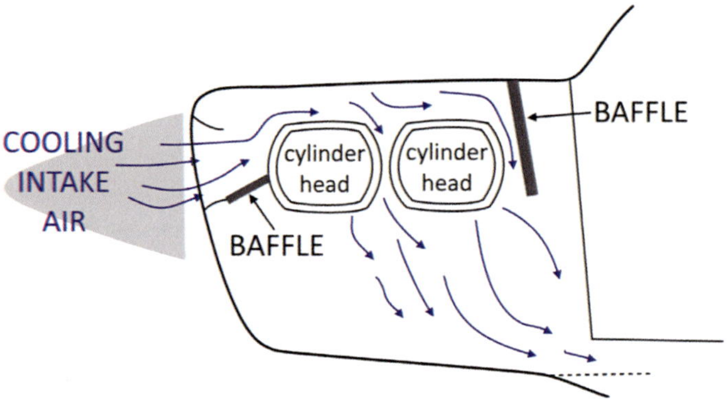

FURTHER READING: APM VOLUME 4, SECTION 2, CHAPTER 20 – THE COOLING SYSTEM

7. **(Answer: B)** The back and forth movement of the pistons is reciprocating motion – hence the name reciprocating engine. To convert this reciprocating motion to rotary, the pistons are attached to the crankshaft via connecting rods or conrods. As the piston is forced back down the cylinder during the power stroke the conrod also moves in such a way as to turn the crankshaft.

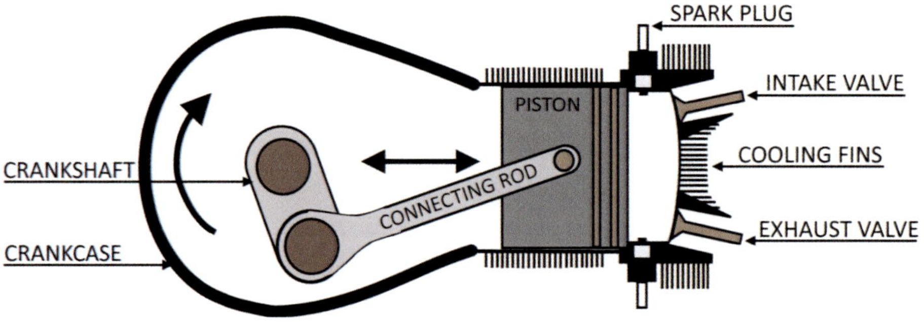

FURTHER READING: APM VOLUME 4, SECTION 2, CHAPTER 16 – THE AEROPLANE ENGINE

8. **(Answer: C)** The camshaft is attached to the crankshaft via a gearing system. It is a reduction gearing system with a 2:1 ratio causing the camshaft to turn once for every two revolutions of the crankshaft, in other words half engine speed.

The camshaft operates the inlet and exhaust valves to the cylinder via push rods and rocker arms. As each valve only needs to open once in every two revolutions of the crankshaft (once in every four strokes of the piston) the camshaft needs to operate at half the speed.

FURTHER READING: APM VOLUME 4, SECTION 2, CHAPTER 16 – THE AEROPLANE ENGINE

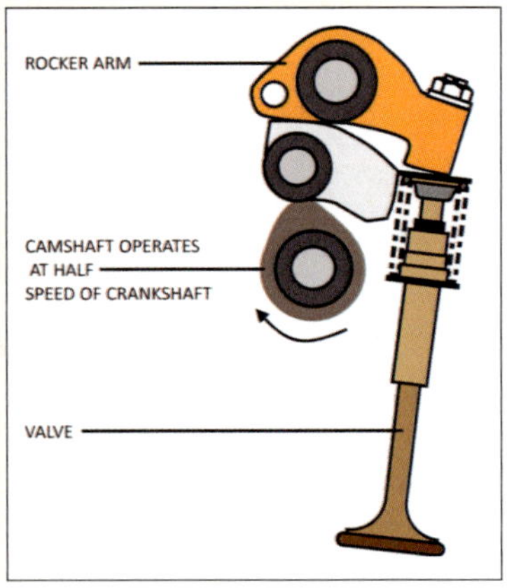

8. ANSWER C

9. **(Answer: D)** In a carburettor the venturi causes the airflow to increase in speed resulting in a drop in pressure (Bernoulli's theorem) in the carburettor throat.

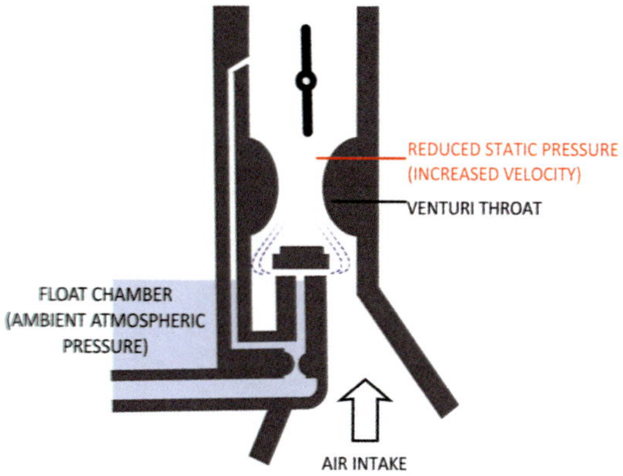

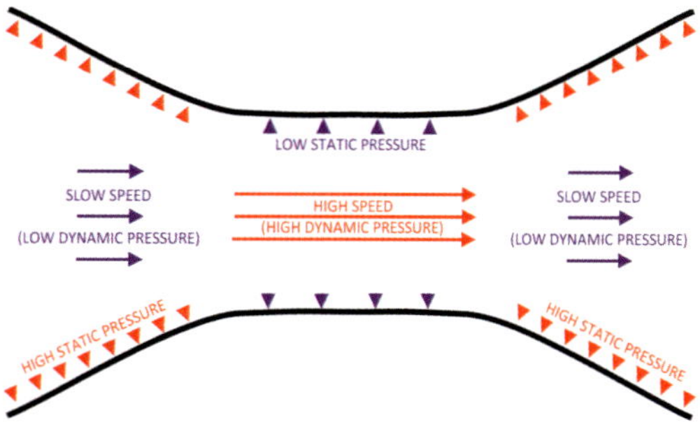

FLOAT TYPE CARBURETTOR

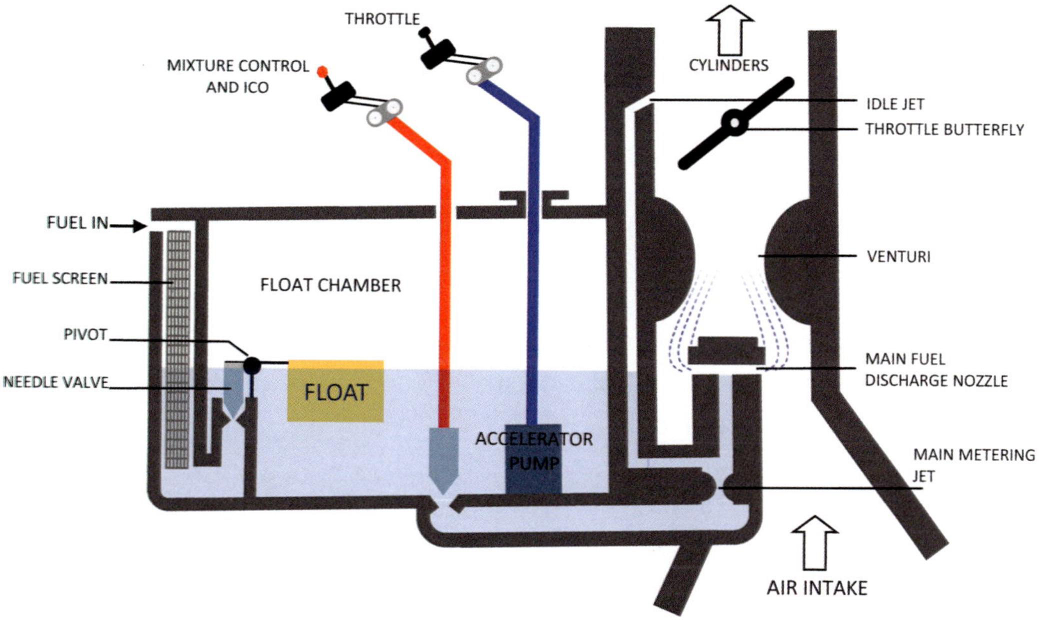

9. ANSWER D

Float Type Carburettor

FLOAT CHAMBER: Fuel level is maintained by a float-type device

MIXTURE NEEDLE: Controls fuel to the discharge nozzle. Its position is adjusted using the mixture control.

DISCHARGE NOZZLE: Fuel is forced into the venturi by the greater ambient atmospheric pressure in the float chamber.

VENTURI: Its shape creates an area of low pressure

THROTTLE VALVE: Controls the flow of the fuel/air mixture. It is adjusted via the throttle control in the cockpit

FURTHER READING: APM VOLUME 4, SECTION 2, CHAPTER 17 – THE CARBURETTOR

10. **(Answer: A)** When the throttle is opened quickly airflow through the carburettor venturi increases at a greater rate than fuel flow, which would lead to an overly weak mixture. The accelerator pump prevents any lag in the power increase by providing an extra spurt of fuel as the throttle is opened.

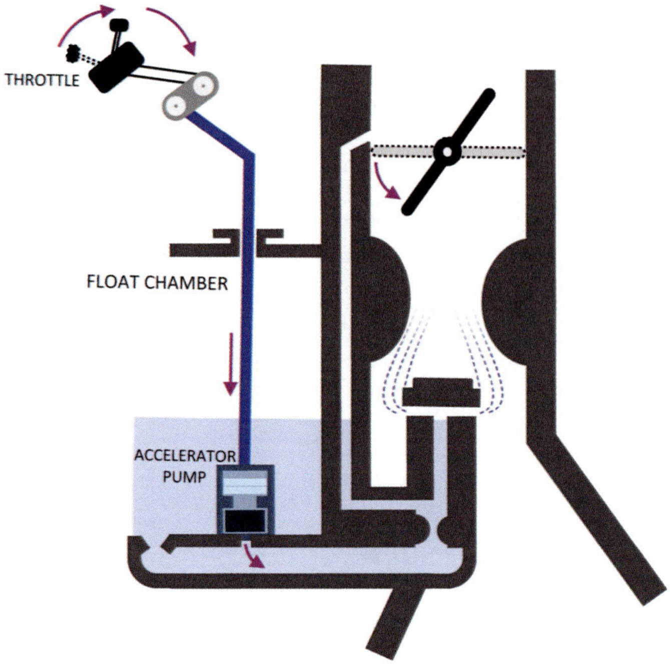

FURTHER READING: APM VOLUME 4, SECTION 2, CHAPTER 17 – THE CARBURETTOR

11. **(Answer: C)** The pressure in the float chamber is the same as the ambient atmospheric pressure. The acceleration of airflow through the venturi causes a decrease in static pressure. The higher pressure in the float chamber forces fuel through the main jet to join the venturi airflow. *(See diagram with Explanation 9, page 19).*

FURTHER READING: APM VOLUME 4, SECTION 2, CHAPTER 17 – THE CARBURETTOR

12. **(Answer: B)** With the engine at idle the butterfly valve is practically closed; in this situation the pressure differential between the venturi and the float chamber will not be sufficient to force fuel through the main jet. To provide sufficient fuel at low rpm an idle jet is located close to the butterfly valve where there is a small venturi effect.

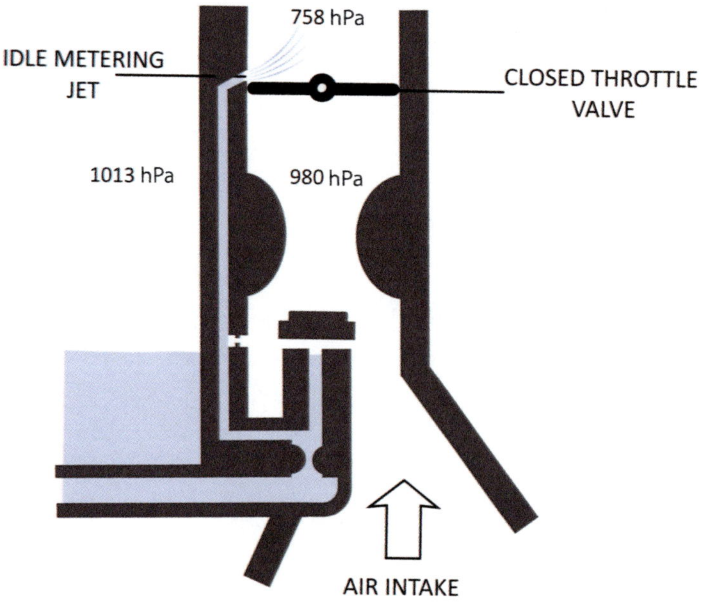

FURTHER READING: APM VOLUME 4, SECTION 2, CHAPTER 17 – THE CARBURETTOR

13. (Answer: D) Causes of engine icing:

EXPANSION: As air accelerates in the venturi the pressure drops and so does the temperature. Warm air can cool rapidly to below zero and if the air is moist enough ice will form.

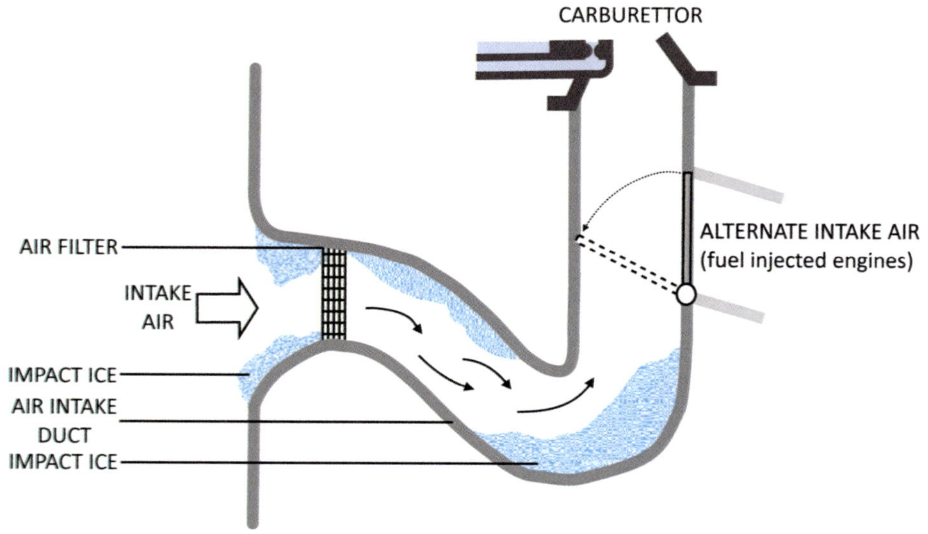

IMPACT ICE: Where super-cooled water droplets in the intake air impact and immediately freeze on the inlet air scoop and the induction to the carburettor. (Note: this type of icing can also affect fuel injected aircraft)

FUEL ICING: Downstream of the jet fuel vaporises absorbing latent heat and leading to a significant drop in temperature. Ice may form on any surface including the inlet walls and the throttle butterfly seriously restricting the airflow to the engine. Fuel icing can occur at temperatures well above freezing, even up to +30°C when the relative humidity is over 50%.

THROTTLE ICING: Occurs when the fuel: air mix accelerates past the throttle butterfly valve resulting in a temperature drop and leading to the possibility of ice forming on the throttle valve. At small throttle openings the acceleration and temperature drop are at their greatest, a situation exacerbated by the fact that at small throttle openings not a great deal of ice is necessary to form a blockage. For this reason there is a greater likelihood of carburettor icing at reduced power settings.

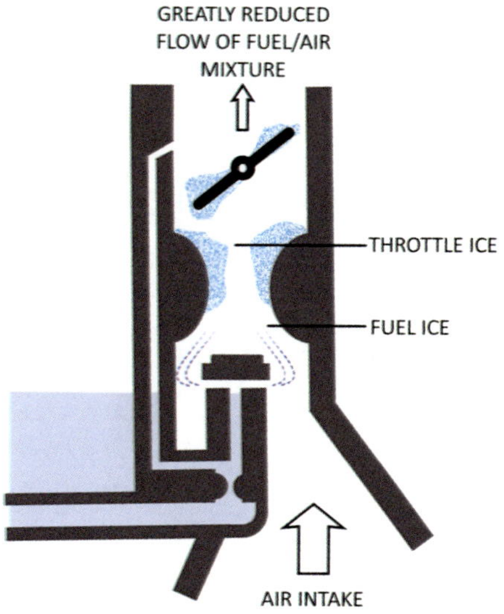

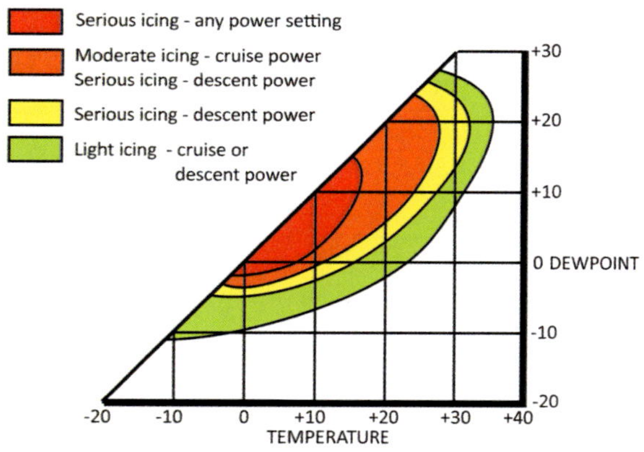

FURTHER READING: APM VOLUME 4, SECTION 2, CHAPTER 17 – THE CARBURETTOR

14. **(Answer: D)** Electric starters have a starter warning light which shows that the starter solenoid is energised and engaged with the engine. If, for some reason, the relay sticks the warning light will remain on, meaning that the starter motor is still engaged with, and is now being driven by, the engine. This could result in very serious damage to both the starter and the engine.

The engine must be shut down immediately if the starter warning light does not go out after the starter is released.

FURTHER READING: APM VOLUME 4, SECTION 2, CHAPTER 16 – THE AEROPLANE ENGINE

15. **(Answer: B)** The high tension supply to the spark plugs is derived from the magneto's self contained generation and distribution system.

FURTHER READING: APM VOLUME 4, SECTION 2, CHAPTER 16 – THE AEROPLANE ENGINE

HOW A MAGNETO WORKS

"Electromagnetism" describes a force that has both an electrical field and a magnetic one; both are therefore intrinsically linked to each other. A changing electrical field generates a magnetic field; conversely a changing magnetic field generates an electrical field. This effect is called electromagnetic induction, and is the basis of operation for a magneto. Because it requires no battery or other source of energy, the magneto is a compact and reliable self-contained ignition system, which is why it is used in many general aviation aircraft.

A magneto consists of a permanent magnet which is rotated close to a conductor; the magnet is turned using ancillary gears from the engine. A coil of wire is wound around the conductor – this is called the primary coil and the rotation of the magnet induces an alternating electrical current to flow within it.

The primary coil consists of around 200 turns of copper wire; one end is permanently grounded to the magneto case, the other is connected to a set of cam-operated breaker points. Usually the breaker points are closed grounding both ends of the primary coil allowing the induced current to flow continuously around the coil.

At the moment of ignition the magneto's cam opens the breaker points, interrupting the current flow in the primary coil and collapsing the magnetic field that has built up around it. This induces a large voltage spike in the primary coil in the region of 200 to 300 volts.

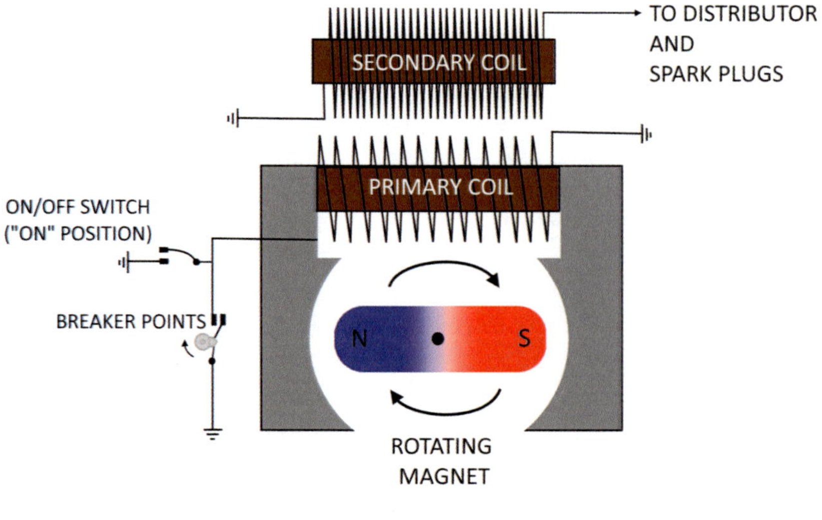

Around the primary coil a second coil of wire is wound (they are depicted as separate in the diagram above for clarity, but are actually wound around the same armature). The second coil is made of thinner wire and has many more turns than the primary (approximately 20,000) making it a kind of step-up transformer. The collapse of the magnetic field around the primary coil induces a high voltage current in the secondary winding. In this way the fairly low primary voltage is converted into a much higher voltage in the secondary circuit, in the order of 20,000 to 30,000 volts, it is this high tension current that is then directed to each spark plug at the appropriate moment.

Every cylinder has two spark plugs and a high voltage spark is timed to occur just before the piston reaches TDC. For increased safety most light aircraft have two magnetos supplying two independent ignition systems. Each system sends high tension voltage to one of the two spark plugs in each cylinder. This arrangement also provides better engine performance as well as redundancy in the event of a failure of one of the magnetos. Under normal circumstances two sparks will provide two flame fronts within the cylinder. The two flame fronts decrease the time needed for the complete fuel charge to start burning, as a result the fuel burns at a lower temperature and pressure.

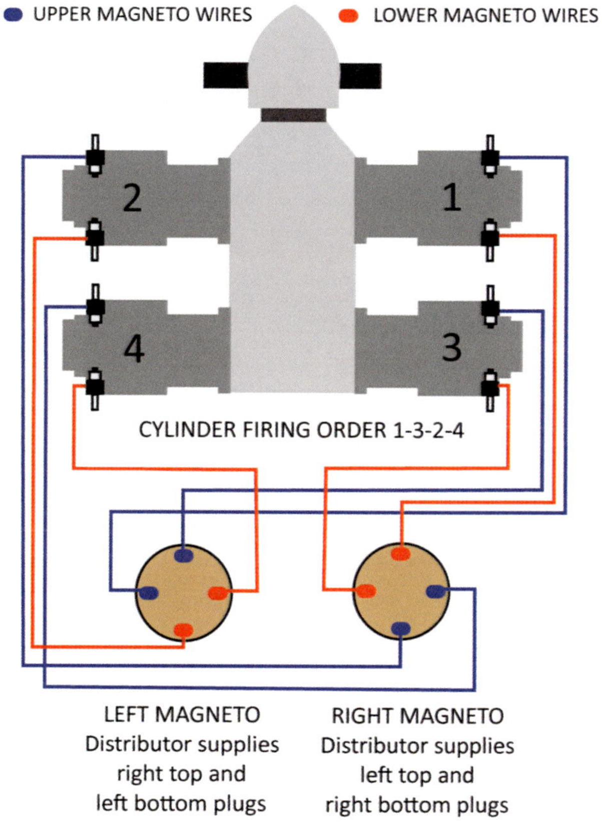

FURTHER READING: APM VOLUME 4, SECTION 2, CHAPTER 16 – THE AEROPLANE ENGINE

16. **(Answer: A)** When the magneto switches are "Off" the switch in the primary circuit is closed and the primary circuit is earthed. This ensures that even if the magnet rotates it cannot induce a voltage in the secondary coil.

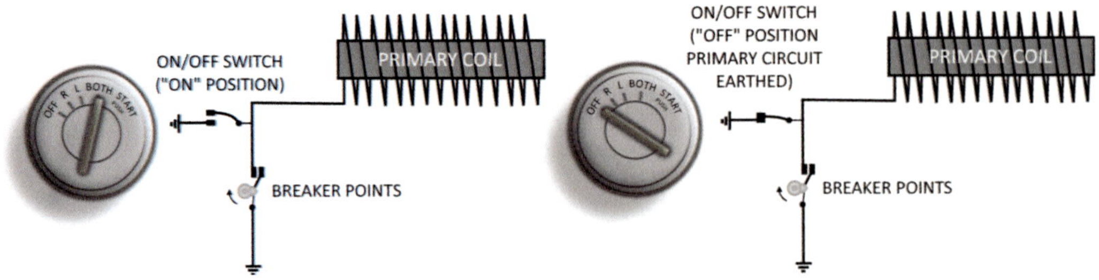

FURTHER READING: APM VOLUME 4, SECTION 2, CHAPTER 16 – THE AEROPLANE ENGINE

17. **(Answer: A)** With the magnetos selected to "Off" the primary circuit is closed, and the low voltage current is sent to earth. This renders the breaker points ineffective and hence no high voltage current can be generated. Should a magneto become detached from the switch it will not earth and the engine will continue to run even when the ignition switch was selected to "Off".

FURTHER READING: APM VOLUME 4, SECTION 2, CHAPTER 16 – THE AEROPLANE ENGINE

18. **(Answer: D)** A magneto is a self-contained electro-magnetic unit driven by the engine camshaft; it is independent of the other aircraft electrical systems.

FURTHER READING: APM VOLUME 4, SECTION 2, CHAPTER 16 – THE AEROPLANE ENGINE

19. **(Answer: D)** V_{NE} is the never exceed speed.

FURTHER READING: APM VOLUME 4, SECTION 3, CHAPTER 25 – PRESSURE INSTRUMENTS

20. **(Answer: C)** Load factors for an aircraft certified in the aerobatic category compared to one certified in the normal or utility category will be higher. Aircraft approved for aerobatics are designed to withstand the stresses imposed by aerobatic manoeuvres. Unlike normal and utility category aircraft, aerobatic aeroplanes must undergo rigorous testing to ensure that they remain controllable throughout a wide range of manoeuvres.

EASA Certification Specifications 23.3 states:

The normal category is limited to non-aerobatic operations. Non-aerobatic operations include –

(1) Any manoeuvre incident to normal flying;

(2) Stalls (except whip stalls); and

(3) Lazy eights, chandelles and steep turns or similar manoeuvres, in which the angle of bank is not more than 60°.

The utility category is limited to any of the operations covered in the normal category; plus -

(1) Spins (if approved for the particular type of aeroplane); and

(2) Lazy eights, chandelles, and steep turns, or similar manoeuvres in which the angle of bank is more than 60° but not more than 90°.

The aerobatic category is without restrictions, other than those shown to be necessary as a result of required flight tests.

FURTHER READING: APM VOLUME 4, SECTION 4, CHAPTER 29 – AIRFRAME LIMITATIONS

END OF EXPLANATIONS PAPER 2

AIRCRAFT GENERAL PAPER 3

1. Detonation may result from using:

   a. Too weak a mixture
   b. Too rich a mixture
   c. A higher fuel grade than usual
   d. Too high a power setting

2. With increase in altitude, air density will ...(i)... if not adjusted the fuel: air mixture will become ...(ii)...:

   a. i) increase ii) weaker
   b. i) increase ii) richer
   c. i) decrease ii) weaker
   d. i) decrease ii) richer

3. Impulse coupling:

   a. Is the means by which the ignition timing is advanced
   b. Is the slow release of stored energy causing the magnet to rotate slowly to generate a high voltage at the spark plug
   c. Is the means by which the rotating magnet is momentarily accelerated to generate a high voltage at the spark plug
   d. Is the rapid release of stored energy causing the magnet to rotate slowly to generate a low voltage at the spark plug

4. To prevent spark plug fouling you should:

   a. Avoid operating the engine at high RPM for long periods of time
   b. Avoid operating the engine at low RPM for long periods of time
   c. Apply power in short bursts when taxiing
   d. Position into wind for pre departure power checks

5. Your aircraft is fitted with a fixed pitch propeller. When accelerating using a constant throttle setting engine speed will:

   a. Decrease
   b. Remain constant
   c. Increase
   d. Remain constant and then slowly decrease

6. To provide an efficient angle of attack throughout the full length of the blade, the blade angle is:

   a. Progressively reduced from hub to tip
   b. Progressively increased from hub to tip
   c. Constant along the length of the blade
   d. Constant to 60% of the blade then reduces to the tip

7. An aeroplane is fitted with a clockwise rotating propeller (when viewed from the pilot's seat); on take-off torque reaction will tend to:

   a. Cause the nose to rise
   b. Cause roll – right wing down
   c. Cause roll – left wing down
   d. Cause the tail to rise

8. What is pre-ignition?

- **a.** A slow but uncontrolled burning of the fuel/air mixture in a hot engine
- **b.** A progressive burning of the fuel/air mixture ahead of the spark from the plug, caused by a hot-spot in the cylinder.
- **c.** An explosive burning of the fuel/air mixture ahead of the spark from the plug, caused by an overly hot engine.
- **d.** An uncontrolled explosion of the fuel/air mixture

9. In a carburettor an accelerator pump:

- **a.** Adds extra fuel to the main jet
- **b.** Prevents excessive fuel being delivered to the cylinders
- **c.** Is a small plunger within the float chamber which is connected to the throttle linkage
- **d.** Ensures the correct volume of fuel is delivered to the cylinders

10. An aeroplane's Certificate of Airworthiness:

- **a.** Is valid for the period specified on the certificate
- **b.** Will not expire under any circumstances
- **c.** Expires after ten years
- **d.** Is valid indefinitely, providing the aircraft is maintained, repaired or modified in an approved manner.

11. A PPL may carry out certain minor repairs and services. Any maintenance carried out by a private pilot:

- **a.** Must be entered in the aircraft logbook if it relates to a primary control system
- **b.** Must be entered in the aircraft logbook and certified by the pilot concerned
- **c.** Must be entered in the aircraft logbook and certified by a licensed engineer
- **d.** Need not be recorded

12. The Airworthiness Requirements (BCAR Section A Chapter 6-2) allow for minor adjustments to be made to a control system while away from base. The second part of the duplicate inspection may be carried out:

- **a.** Only by the captain of the aircraft
- **b.** By an engineer licensed on the aircraft type concerned
- **c.** When the aircraft returns to base
- **d.** By a pilot licensed for the aircraft type concerned

13. A PPL may carry out certain minor repairs and services, these are:

- **a.** Listed in the Air Navigation (General) Regulations. The aeroplane concerned must be less than 5,700 kg
- **b.** Listed in the Pilot's Operating Handbook. The aeroplane concerned must be less than 2,730kg
- **c.** Listed in the Air Navigation (General) Regulations. The aeroplane concerned must be less than 2,730 kg and not used for public transport
- **d.** Listed in the Certificate of Maintenance Review. The aeroplane concerned must be less than 5,700 kg and not used for public transport

14. Any defects requiring maintenance which are encountered during a flight should be recorded by the pilot:

- **a.** On the Certificate of Maintenance Review
- **b.** In the Aircraft Technical Log
- **c.** On the Certificate of Release to Service
- **d.** On any handy scrap of paper which should be left in the aircraft

15. Before a flight, the legal responsibility to ensure that all of an aircraft's maintenance documentation is current rests with the:

- **a.** Pilot
- **b.** Aircraft Owner
- **c.** Aircraft Operator
- **d.** Chief Engineer

16. The green arc on the airspeed indicator shows the:

- **a.** Flap operating range
- **b.** Caution range
- **c.** V_{NE} range
- **d.** Normal operating range

17. The yellow arc on the airspeed indicator shows the:

- **a.** Caution range
- **b.** Normal operating range
- **c.** Flap operating range
- **d.** V_{NE} range

18. For an aircraft in flight the pressure entering the forward facing hole of a pitot tube is:

- **a.** Dynamic pressure plus pitot pressure
- **b.** Dynamic pressure
- **c.** Static pressure
- **d.** Dynamic pressure and static pressure

19. A Vertical Speed Indicator works by measuring:

- **a.** The difference between static and dynamic pressure
- **b.** The rate of change in the difference between static and dynamic pressure
- **c.** The time between particular levels in a climb or descent
- **d.** Rate of change of static pressure

20. On the ground the weight of an aircraft is balanced by the reaction force of the ground on the aircraft which acts:

- **a.** Upwards through the tailplane
- **b.** Upwards through the wheels
- **c.** Downwards through the wheels
- **d.** Parallel to the ground through the engine and propeller

END OF AIRCRAFT GENERAL PAPER 3

AIRCRAFT GENERAL
PAPER 3: ANSWERS

No	A	B	C	D
1	X			
2				X
3			X	
4		X		
5			X	
6	X			
7			X	
8		X		
9			X	
10				X
11		X		
12				X
13			X	
14		X		
15	X			
16				X
17	X			
18				X
19				X
20		X		

CORRECT ANSWERS: PERCENTAGES					
15	16	17	18	19	20
75%	80%	85%	90%	95%	100%

1. **(Answer: A)** Detonation will occur if too weak a mixture is used. Combine this with high cylinder head temperatures (fuel is also a cooling agent in the engine) and the fuel: air mix can spontaneously ignite and burn in a violent and uncontrolled manner. The explosive increase in pressure that is created can cause severe damage to the engine, possibly even leading to failure of the engine.

   You would detect detonation by the engine running roughly and an increase in cylinder head temperatures. Corrective action is to:
   - *Enrichen the mixture*
   - *Throttle back (reduce pressure in the cylinders)*
   - *Increase airspeed to aid cooling*

   Apart from an overly lean mixture, other factors that can lead to detonation are:
   - *Using a lower grade of fuel than recommended*
   - *Using time-expired fuel*
   - *An over-heated engine*
   - *Excessive manifold pressure*

FURTHER READING: APM VOLUME 4, SECTION 2, CHAPTER 17 – THE CARBURETTOR

2. **(Answer: D)** With increase in altitude, air density reduces and if not adjusted the fuel: air mixture will become richer. An overly rich mixture will lead to the engine running roughly and if not corrected possibly a rich cut.

FURTHER READING: APM VOLUME 4, SECTION 2, CHAPTER 17 – THE CARBURETTOR

3. **(Answer: C)** Impulse coupling accelerates the rotating magnet momentarily to generate a high voltage; it also retards the ignition timing at low RPM until after top dead centre. After start the timing of the spark returns to just before top dead centre.

FURTHER READING: APM VOLUME 4, SECTION 2, CHAPTER 16 – THE AEROPLANE ENGINE

4. **(Answer: B)** Spark plug fouling can be prevented by not operating at low RPM for long periods of time. When operating at low engine RPM the combustion of the fuel: air mixture is not efficient as the engine is not at its optimum operating temperature. Unburned fuel can cause carbon deposits to build up, especially on the spark plug electrodes and exhaust valves. The build up on the spark plugs can lead to rough running and misfiring.

FURTHER READING: APM VOLUME 4, SECTION 2, CHAPTER 16 – THE AEROPLANE ENGINE

5. **(Answer: C)** On an aircraft with a fixed pitch propeller as the speed increases the engine RPM will also increase even though the throttle setting remains unchanged.

FURTHER READING: APM VOLUME 4, SECTION 2, CHAPTER 21 – ENGINE HANDLING

6. **(Answer: A)** Ideally a propeller should produce uniform thrust along the length of the blade. Therefore the blade is twisted so that the blade angle, and hence the angle of attack, reduces from hub to tip. The result is that the faster moving parts of the propeller have a smaller angle of attack and the slower segments have a larger angle of attack, hence overall the thrust is even along the length of the blade.

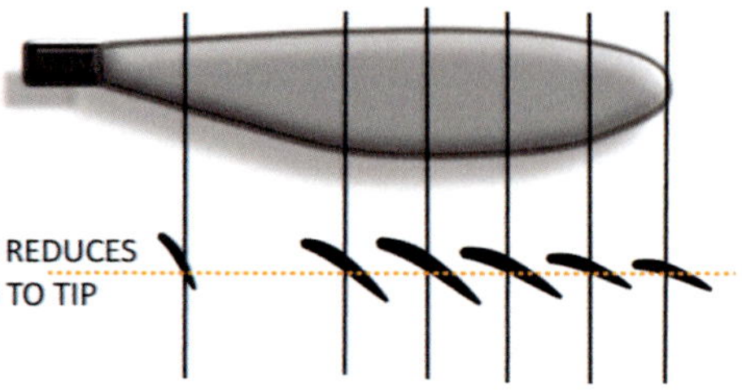

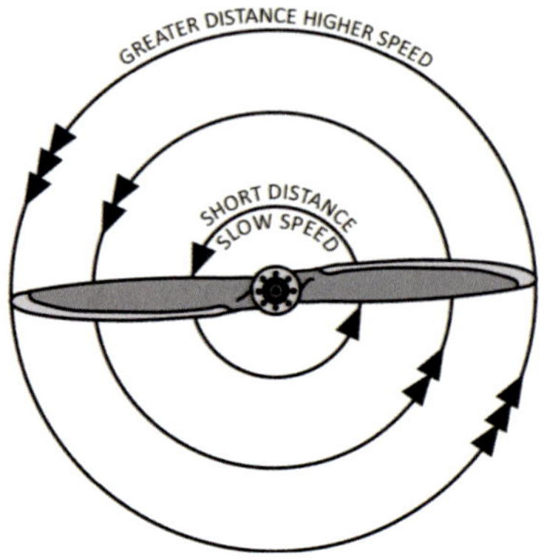

FURTHER READING: APM VOLUME 4, SECTION 2, CHAPTER 21 – ENGINE HANDLING

7. **(Answer: C)** If the propeller rotates clockwise (when viewed from behind) torque reaction will tend to rotate the aircraft anti-clockwise and roll it to the left.

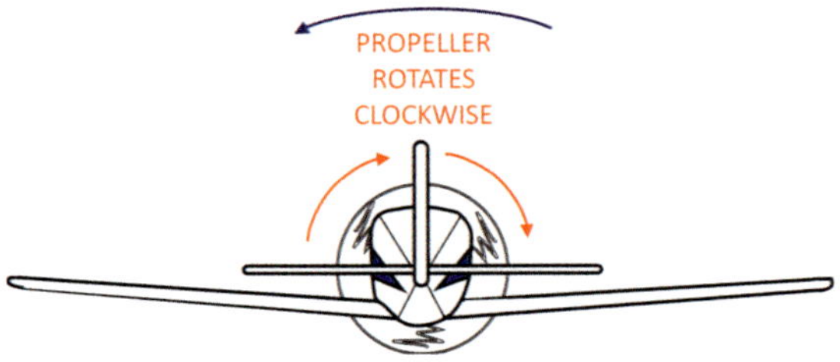

FURTHER READING: APM VOLUME 4, SECTION 2, CHAPTER 21 – ENGINE HANDLING

8. **(Answer: B)** Pre-ignition is the progressive burning of the fuel: air mixture occurring in advance of the spark from the plug. It can be caused by a hot-spot, usually a carbon deposit in the cylinder becoming red hot and igniting the mixture. The effect would be rough running, perhaps back firing and a rise in cylinder head temperature. A possible cause is using high power with too lean a mixture meaning that there is no excess fuel to provide cooling.

FURTHER READING: APM VOLUME 4, SECTION 2, CHAPTER 17 – THE CARBURETTOR

9. **(Answer: C)** The accelerator pump is a small plunger within the float chamber, it is attached to the throttle linkage. When the throttle is opened quickly airflow through the carburettor venturi increases at a greater rate than fuel flow, which would lead to an overly weak mixture. The accelerator pump prevents any lag in the power increase by providing an extra spurt of fuel as the throttle is opened. *(See diagrams on pages 19 and 20).*

FURTHER READING: APM VOLUME 4, SECTION 2, CHAPTER 17 – THE CARBURETTOR

10. **(Answer: D)** EASA Certificates of Airworthiness are non-expiring, provided that the aircraft is modified, repaired and maintained in an approved manner. Aircraft governed by EASA must be maintained in accordance with a Light Aircraft Maintenance Program (LAMP). *Note: Annex 2 aircraft would have a C of A issued for 3 years only.*

FURTHER READING: APM VOLUME 4, SECTION 4, CHAPTER 28 – AIRWORTHINESS

11. **(Answer: B)** Owners or aircraft operators holding a PPL or higher are allowed to carry out minor repairs or servicing on their aircraft. The legislation is set out in the ANO Article 16(7). Pilots should record any minor work carried out in the appropriate logbook and certify it with their licence number and signature.

FURTHER READING: APM VOLUME 4, SECTION 4, CHAPTER 28 – AIRWORTHINESS

12. **(Answer: D)** In order for an aircraft to be considered airworthy again following any adjustments made to either the flight controls and/or the engine controls an inspection must be made by two licensed personnel, either engineers or inspectors. However, the Airworthiness Requirements (BCAR Section A Chapter 6-2) allow for minor adjustments to be made to a control system while the aircraft is away from base and for the second part of the Duplicate Inspection to be carried out by a pilot licensed for the type of aircraft concerned.

FURTHER READING: APM VOLUME 4, SECTION 4, CHAPTER 28 – AIRWORTHINESS

13. **(Answer: C)** Owners or aircraft operators holding a PPL or higher are allowed to carry out minor repairs or servicing on their aircraft. The minor repairs and replacements permitted are listed in the Air Navigation (General) Regulations Part 4. The aeroplane concerned must weigh less than 2,730 kg and must not used for public transport.

FURTHER READING: APM VOLUME 4, SECTION 4, CHAPTER 28 – AIRWORTHINESS

14. **(Answer: B)** Pilots should review the Tech Log, as well as the Airworthiness Review Certificate (or in the case of an Annex 2 aircraft, the Certificate of Maintenance Review) and the Certificate of Release to Service prior to flight.

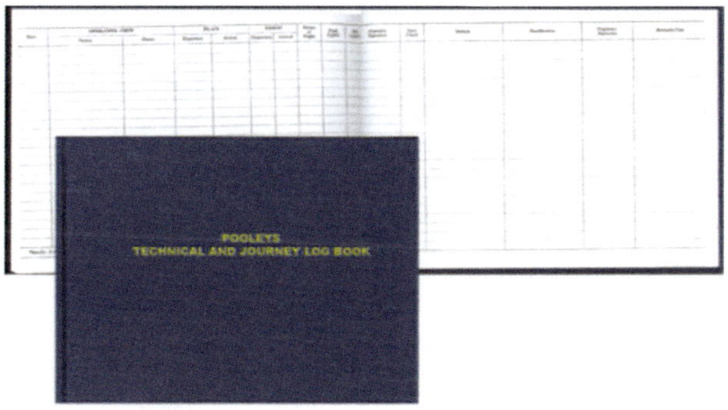

FURTHER READING: APM VOLUME 4, SECTION 4, CHAPTER 28 – AIRWORTHINESS

15. **(Answer: A)** Prior to flight it is legally the pilot's responsibility to ensure that the aircraft's maintenance documentation is current and correct.

FURTHER READING: APM VOLUME 4, SECTION 4, CHAPTER 28 – AIRWORTHINESS

16. **(Answer: D)** The green arc on the ASI denotes the normal operating range. It extends from the stall speed at maximum all up weight with gear and flap retracted V_{SI} to V_{NO}, the maximum structural cruising speed, a speed which should not be exceeded except in smooth air. At all speeds within the green arc it will be safe to operate in any conditions.

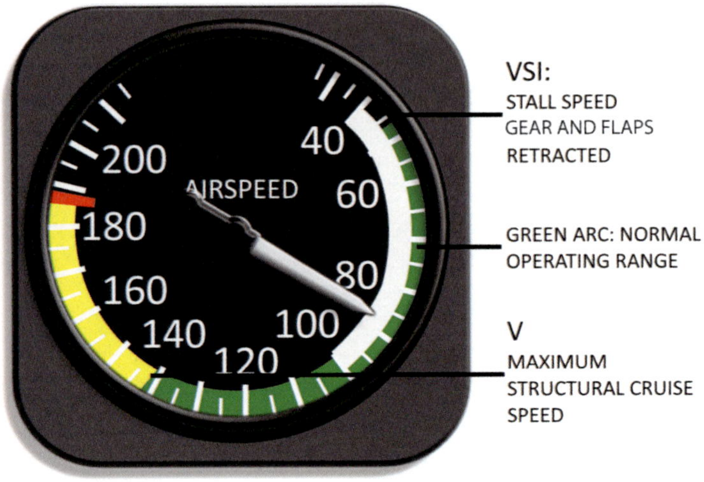

FURTHER READING: APM VOLUME 4, SECTION 3, CHAPTER 25 – PRESSURE INSTRUMENTS

17. **(Answer: A)** The yellow arc on the ASI denotes the caution range. It extends from V_{NO}, the normal operating limit speed, to V_{NE} the never exceed speed. Operations within the yellow caution range should only be undertaken in smooth air.

V -SPEEDS:

V_{SO} – stalling speed, gear down, flaps lowered, power off
V_{SI} – stalling speed, gear up, flaps up, power off
V_{FE} – maximum speed for extending flap
V_{NO} – maximum structural cruise speed
V_{NE} – never exceed speed

FURTHER READING: APM VOLUME 4, SECTION 3, CHAPTER 25 – PRESSURE INSTRUMENTS

18. **(Answer: D)** The pitot tube measures total (or pitot) pressure, that is both dynamic pressure and static pressure. Dynamic pressure is the result of forward motion, but static pressure is omnipresent.

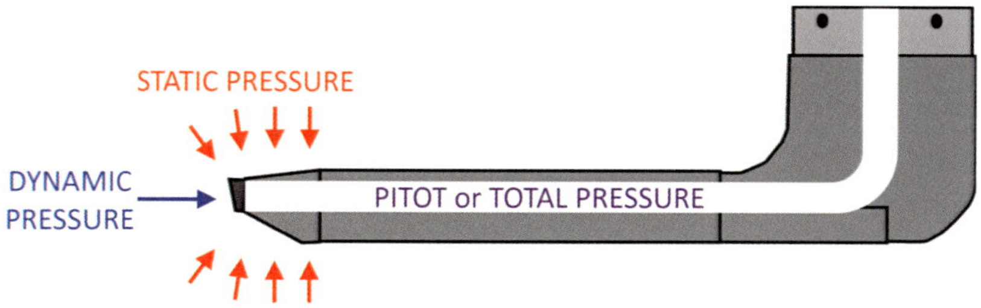

FURTHER READING: APM VOLUME 4, SECTION 3, CHAPTER 25 – PRESSURE INSTRUMENTS

19. **(Answer: D)** A Vertical Speed Indicator works by measuring the rate of change of static pressure. Within the VSI is a capsule into which static pressure is fed. Static pressure also enters the instrument casing surrounding the capsule; the difference is that this static source is routed through restriction so that it is delayed on entering the casing.

In level flight the pressures within and outside the capsule will be equal, there is no pressure differential and the VSI will indicate zero. When a climb is commenced the static pressure inside the capsule will start to fall immediately. However, the static pressure outside the capsule is metered and will not change as rapidly. Consequently the capsule will contract slightly as the pressure is now higher outside the capsule than inside. The capsule movement is translated via linkages in the instrument to show a rate of climb.

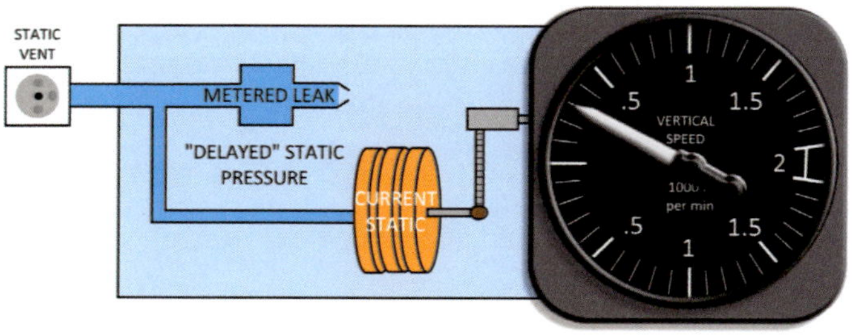

FURTHER READING: APM VOLUME 4, SECTION 3, CHAPTER 25 – PRESSURE INSTRUMENTS

20. **(Answer: B)** While on the ground the aeroplane's weight is balanced by the reaction force of the ground on the aircraft, which acts upwards through the wheels.

FURTHER READING: APM VOLUME 4, SECTION 1, CHAPTER 2 – WEIGHT

END OF EXPLANATIONS PAPER 3

INTENTIONALLY BLANK

AIRCRAFT GENERAL PAPER 4

1. Dynamic pressure is found in the ASI by:

a. Subtracting pitot tube pressure from static line pressure
b. Adding static line pressure and pitot tube pressure
c. Subtracting total pressure from static line pressure
d. Subtracting static line pressure from pitot tube pressure

2. During flight you suspect that the static line may be blocked and elect to use the alternate static source. When compared to the main static source, alternate static pressure is:

a. Higher
b. Lower
c. The same
d. Either higher or lower depending on the ambient pressure

3. Within an altimeter:

a. As the aircraft climbs the aneroid capsule inside contracts. The movement is transmitted to a pointer via appropriate linkages which moves around the scale of the instrument.
b. Static line pressure is connected to the aneroid capsule; pitot pressure is connected to the capsule surrounding the capsule.
c. As the aircraft descends the aneroid capsule inside contracts. The movement is transmitted to a pointer via appropriate linkages which moves around the scale of the instrument.
d. Pitot pressure is connected to the aneroid capsule; static line pressure is connected to the capsule surrounding the capsule.

4. During descent the static supply to the altimeter and airspeed indicator becomes blocked. The result is that:

a. Both the altimeter and ASI will over-read
b. The altimeter will over-read and the ASI under-read
c. Both the altimeter and ASI will under-read
d. The altimeter will under-read and the ASI will over-read

5. A Vertical Speed Indicator indicates:

a. Rate of change of altitude in feet per minute
b. Rate of change of speed in feet per minute
c. Rate of change of altitude in knots
d. Rate of change of speed in knots

6. A Vertical Speed Indicator converts rate of change of ...(i)... to a rate of change of ...(ii)...

a. i) pitot ii) altitude
b. i) pitot ii) speed
c. i) static ii) altitude
d. i) static ii) speed

7. Gyroscopes are used in the:

a. Attitude Indicator, Airspeed Indicator, Turn Coordinator and Direction Indicator
b. Attitude Indicator, Turn Coordinator and Direction Indicator
c. Altimeter, Turn Coordinator, and Attitude Indicator
d. Altimeter, Turn Coordinator and Heading Indicator

8. A gyroscope possesses a property called "rigidity in space". Which of the following best describes the factors controlling the degree of rigidity displayed by a gyroscope?

- **a.** The speed of rotation and the position of its centre of gravity
- **b.** The speed of rotation, the rotor mass and the position of its centre of pressure
- **c.** The speed of rotation, the rotor mass and the position of its centre of gravity
- **d.** The speed of rotation and the rotor mass

9. The gyroscope in an Artificial Horizon is:

- **a.** A tied gyro rotating in the vertical plane around the horizontal axis
- **b.** A space gyro rotating in the vertical plane around the horizontal axis
- **c.** An earth gyro rotating in the horizontal plane around the vertical axis
- **d.** A space gyro rotating in the horizontal plane around the vertical axis

10. The Direction Indicator suffers from apparent drift due to:

- **a.** The spin axis of the gyroscope moving
- **b.** Errors within the instrument
- **c.** Changes in the rotor RPM
- **d.** The rotation of the earth

11. The Direction Indicator should be aligned with the magnetic compass every 10 to 15 minutes when:

- **a.** The aircraft is in unaccelerated straight and level flight
- **b.** The aircraft is in a level coordinated turn
- **c.** The aircraft is in a steady, coordinated descent
- **d.** The aircraft is in a balanced climb

12. A compass deviation card is necessary to show:

- **a.** The correction to be applied to the compass reading to obtain compass heading
- **b.** The correction to be applied to the compass reading to obtain magnetic heading
- **c.** The correction to be applied to the magnetic heading to obtain true heading
- **d.** The correction to be applied to the compass reading to obtain true heading

13. A monocoque structure is one where:

- **a.** There is an internal structure but stresses are mostly carried by the skin
- **b.** There is no internal structure and stresses are carried by the skin
- **c.** There is no internal structure and stresses are carried by formers
- **d.** There is an internal structure and stresses are carried by formers

14. A semi-monocoque structure is one where:

- **a.** There is a heavy duty framework covered with an aluminium skin
- **b.** There is a light framework covered by an aluminium skin
- **c.** There is a heavy duty framework covered with a doped fabric skin
- **d.** There is a light framework covered with a doped fabric skin

15. Identify the component parts of a wing structure indicated:

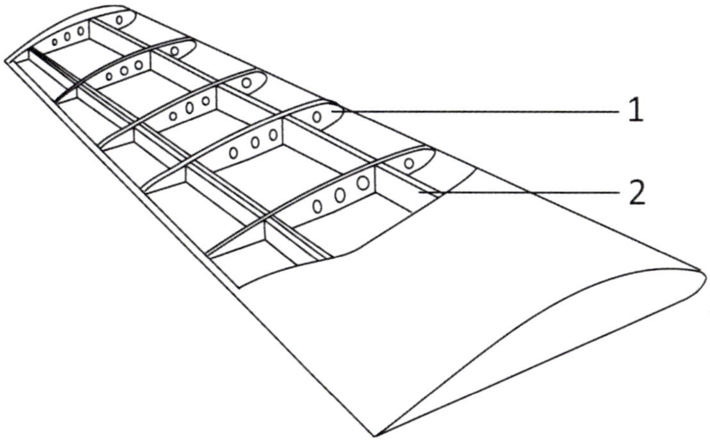

a. 1. Former 2. Main Spar
b. 1. Rib 2. Primary Spar
c. 1. Rib 2. Main Spar
d. 1. Former 2. Stringer

16. Flying control locks are used:

a. On the ground to ensure that the control surfaces are not damaged in high winds
b. In the air in the event of the failure of rigging to a control surface
c. On the ground to ensure that the trim tabs are not damaged in high winds
d. In the air to ease the pilot's workload

17. Wing spars carry the major loads experienced by the wing. Where lift is generated these are ...(i)... bending loads, where the fuselage and fuel tanks are supported they are ...(ii)... bending loads.

a. i) downward ii) downward
b. i) downward ii) upward
c. i) upward ii) downward
d. i) upward ii) upward

18. A pilot can identify tyre creep using:

a. Two opposing arrows painted on the side wall of the tyre
b. Two alignment marks, one painted on the tyre side wall and one on the wheel flange
c. Two opposing arrows painted on the wheel flange
d. A pressure check together with checking the condition of the inflation valve

19. With regard to a magnetic compass, which of the following statements are true?

1. A magnetic compass does not suffer from turning or acceleration errors
2. The fluid within the compass supports the weight of the magnet, decreases friction and dampens oscillations
3. The aeroplane moves around the compass magnet
4. When deviation is applied to the compass heading we get the magnetic heading
5. When variation is applied to the compass heading we get the magnetic heading

The correct statements are:

a. 2, 3 and 5
b. 1, 2 and 4
c. 2, 3 and 4
d. 1, 4 and 5

20. During a pre-flight inspection of the brakes one important item to check is:

a. That the discs are pitted
b. The brake assembly is nice and loose
c. That the brake discs are not corroded
d. There is no need to inspect the brake assembly, it is done during the 50 hour check

END OF AIRCRAFT GENERAL PAPER 4

INTENTIONALLY BLANK

AIRCRAFT GENERAL
PAPER 4: ANSWERS

No	A	B	C	D
1				X
2		X		
3			X	
4	X			
5	X			
6			X	
7		X		
8			X	
9			X	
10				X
11	X			
12		X		
13		X		
14		X		
15			X	
16	X			
17			X	
18		X		
19			X	
20			X	

CORRECT ANSWERS: PERCENTAGES					
15	16	17	18	19	20
75%	80%	85%	90%	95%	100%

1. **(Answer: D)** Dynamic pressure is found in the ASI by subtracting static line pressure from pitot pressure. This is achieved by feeding total pressure, the pressure measurement from the pitot, into an expandable diaphragm and static line pressure into the capsule around the diaphragm.

   PITOT PRESSURE (dynamic + static) – STATIC PRESSURE = DYNAMIC PRESSURE

   As airspeed rises, the dynamic pressure increases, however static pressure remains unchanged. The diaphragm expands with the rise in dynamic pressure and through a series of gears a pointer is positioned to represent the increase in airspeed.

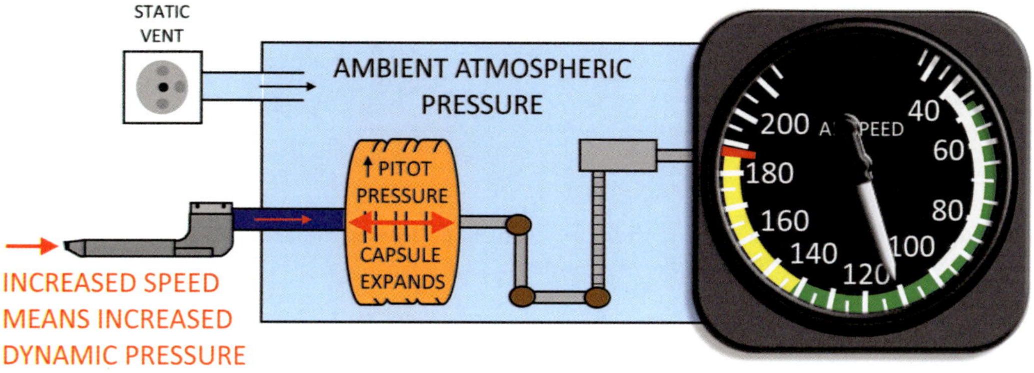

FURTHER READING: APM VOLUME 4, SECTION 3, CHAPTER 25 – PRESSURE INSTRUMENTS

2. **(Answer: B)** The alternate static source is taken from within the cabin, this pressure is usually slightly lower than external atmospheric pressure. Using alternate static will mean that the instrument readings will not be as accurate.

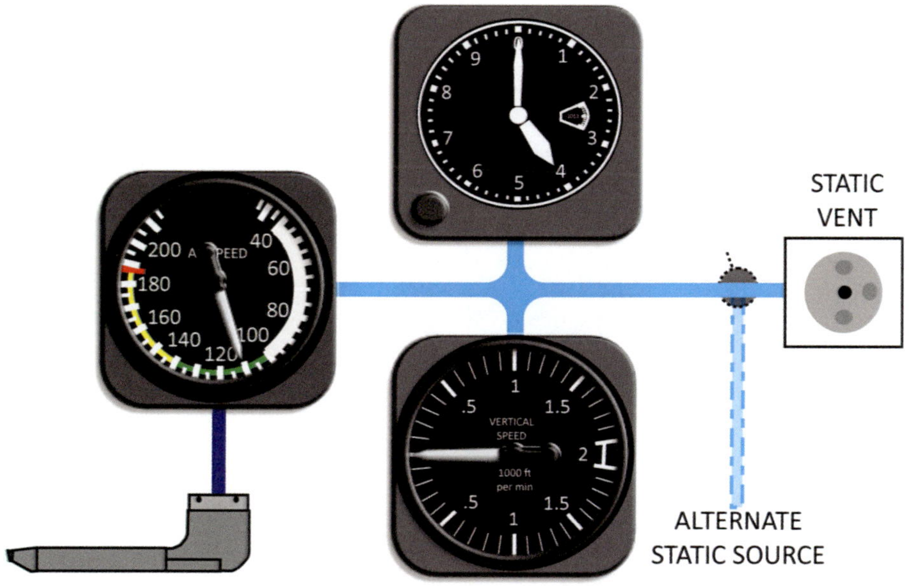

FURTHER READING: APM VOLUME 4, SECTION 3, CHAPTER 25 – PRESSURE INSTRUMENTS

3. **(Answer: C)** As the aircraft descends the aneroid capsule inside the altimeter contracts, pushed inwards by rising ambient pressure around it. The movement is transmitted to a pointer via appropriate linkages which move needles around the scale of the instrument.

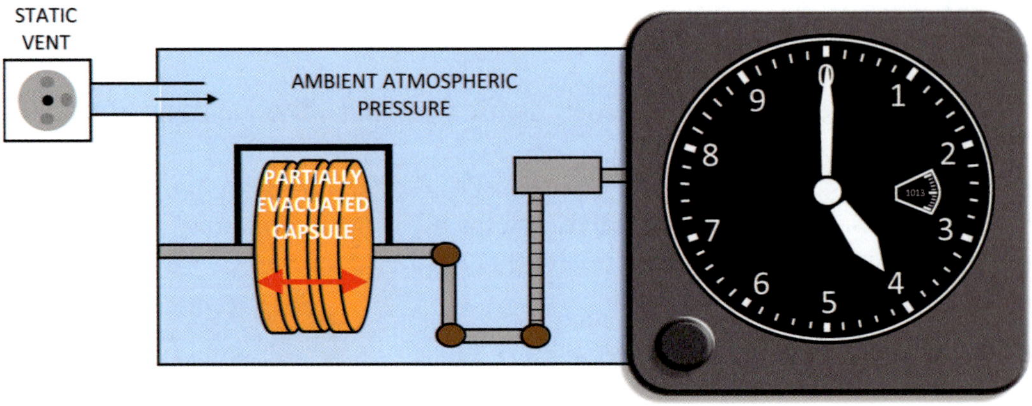

FURTHER READING: APM VOLUME 4, SECTION 3, CHAPTER 25 – PRESSURE INSTRUMENTS

4. **(Answer: A)** During descent the static supply to the altimeter and airspeed indicator becomes blocked. The result is that both the altimeter and ASI will over-read.

Altimeter: will continue to measure the static pressure trapped in the line and so will indicate the level at which the blockage occurred. Thus in a descent it will over-read.

ASI: A blocked static vent would cause the ASI to over-read. The static pressure trapped in the line will be lower than the actual pressure as the aircraft descends. The measured difference between the pitot pressure and the static pressure will be more than actual; hence the ASI will indicate a higher airspeed than is really being achieved.

For the sake of completeness, the VSI will indicate zero should a blockage of the static supply occur during level flight.

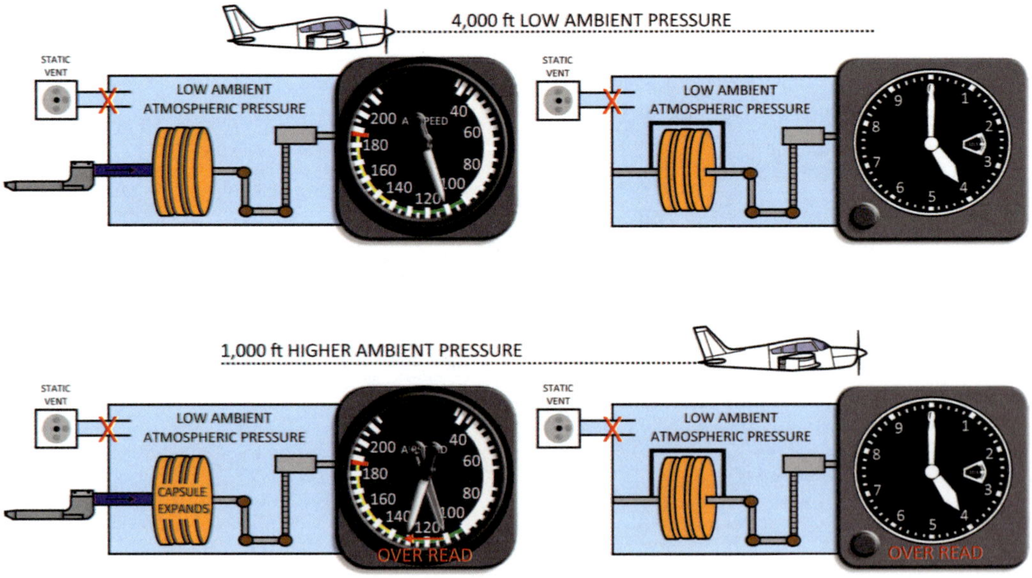

FURTHER READING: APM VOLUME 4, SECTION 3, CHAPTER 25 – PRESSURE INSTRUMENTS

5. **(Answer: A)** A Vertical Speed Indicator (VSI) indicates rate of change of altitude in feet per minute. Within the VSI is a capsule into which static pressure is fed. Static pressure also enters the instrument casing surrounding the capsule; the difference is that this static source is routed through a restriction so that it is delayed on entering the casing.

   In level flight the pressures within and outside the capsule will be equal, there is no pressure differential and the VSI will indicate zero. When a climb is commenced the static pressure inside the capsule will start to fall immediately, however the static pressure outside the capsule is metered and will not change as rapidly. Consequently the capsule will contract slightly as the pressure is now higher outside the capsule than inside. The capsule movement is translated via linkages in the instrument to show a rate of climb.

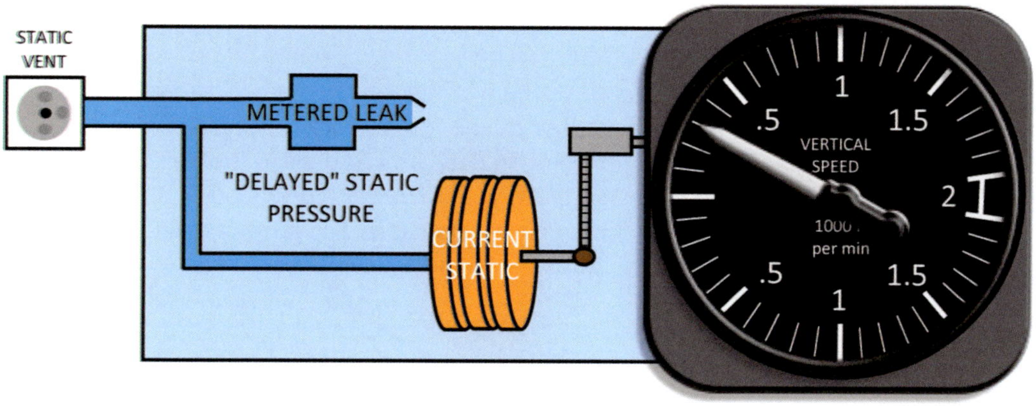

FURTHER READING: APM VOLUME 4, SECTION 3, CHAPTER 25 – PRESSURE INSTRUMENTS

6. **(Answer: C)** A Vertical Speed Indicator converts rate of change of static pressure to a rate of change of altitude.

FURTHER READING: APM VOLUME 4, SECTION 3, CHAPTER 25 – PRESSURE INSTRUMENTS

7. **(Answer: B)** Gyroscopes are used in the Attitude Indicator, Turn Coordinator and Direction Indicator.

FURTHER READING: APM VOLUME 4, SECTION 3, CHAPTER 26 – GYROSCOPIC INSTRUMENTS

8. **(Answer: C)** A gyroscope is a rotating wheel mounted on gimbals so that it is able to turn freely in one or more directions as required. A rotating mass is able to maintain the same absolute direction in space independent of what is going on around it. This property is called "rigidity in space". In other words the gyroscope remains stable as the aircraft moves around it.

   The degree of rigidity depends upon:

   - The rotor mass
   - The speed of rotation and
   - The radius at which the mass is concentrated (its centre of gravity)

FURTHER READING: APM VOLUME 4, SECTION 3, CHAPTER 26 – GYROSCOPIC INSTRUMENTS

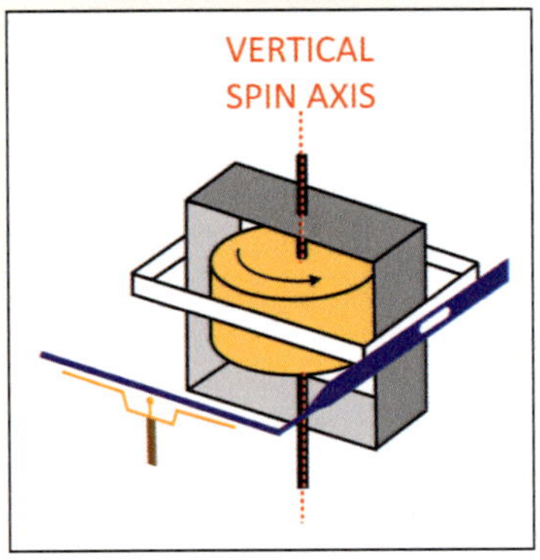

9. ANSWER C

9. **(Answer: C)** The gyroscope in an Attitude Indicator is an earth gyro rotating in the horizontal plane around the vertical axis. The attitude indicator displays a miniature aircraft and horizon bar, providing the pilot with a picture representing the attitude of the aircraft. The instrument gives an instantaneous indication of changes in attitude. Attitude indicators use a gyroscope (powered either by a vacuum pump or an electrical motor) to establish an inertial reference platform.

The gyro in the attitude indicator is mounted in a horizontal plane and depends upon rigidity in space for its operation. The instrument's horizon bar is fixed to the gyro and represents the true horizon, it remains in an earth horizontal plane as the aircraft is pitched or banked about its lateral or longitudinal axis. In other words, the aircraft actually rotates around the spinning gyro.

FURTHER READING: APM VOLUME 4, SECTION 3, CHAPTER 26 – GYROSCOPIC INSTRUMENTS

10. **(Answer: D)** Apparent wander is caused by the rotation of the earth. The gyroscope is aligned with a point in space, not a point on the earth. As the earth rotates the gyro will continue to point at its original reference point. From the pilot's point of view the DI appears to change heading even though a constant direction is maintained.

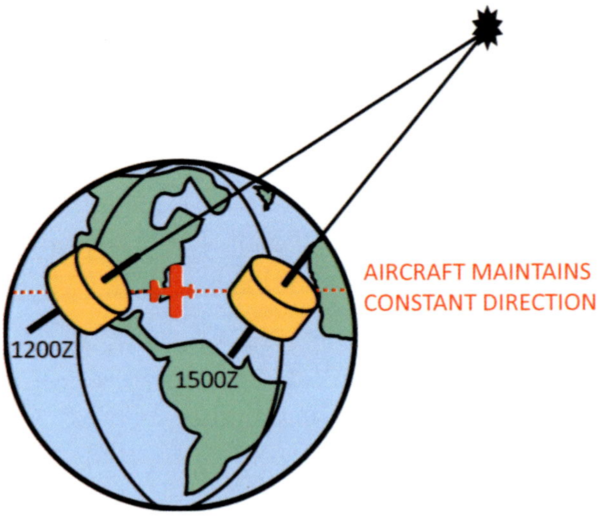

Real wander is caused by mechanical imperfections with the instrument; for example worn bearings, friction, or the gyroscope not being in perfect balance.

FURTHER READING: APM VOLUME 4, SECTION 3, CHAPTER 26 – GYROSCOPIC INSTRUMENTS

11. **(Answer: A)** The DI should be periodically checked against the magnetic compass. This should be done when the compass is not experiencing any errors; compass errors will be caused when turning or changing speed. Therefore the DI should be adjusted when the aircraft is in unaccelerated straight and level flight.

FURTHER READING: APM VOLUME 4, SECTION 3, CHAPTER 26 – GYROSCOPIC INSTRUMENTS

12. **(Answer: B)** A compass will be affected not only by the earth's magnetic field, but also any other magnetic field, such as may be generated by radios, engines etc..

The combined effect of these magnetic fields is called deviation; it is a measure of how much the compass is made to deviate from magnetic north. Each aircraft will have a deviation card which will show the correction that needs to be applied to a compass reading to obtain the magnetic heading.

FURTHER READING: APM VOLUME 4, SECTION 3, CHAPTER 27 – THE MAGNETIC COMPASS

13. (Answer: B) A monocoque structure is one where there is no internal structure and stresses are carried by the skin. The classic example of a monocoque structure is an egg.

FURTHER READING: APM VOLUME 4, SECTION 2, CHAPTER 15 – THE AIRFRAME

14. (Answer: B) A semi-monocoque structure is one where there is a light framework covered by an aluminium skin that carries most of the stress.

FURTHER READING: APM VOLUME 4, SECTION 2, CHAPTER 15 – THE AIRFRAME

15. (Answer: C) The parts are: 1. Rib 2. Main Spar

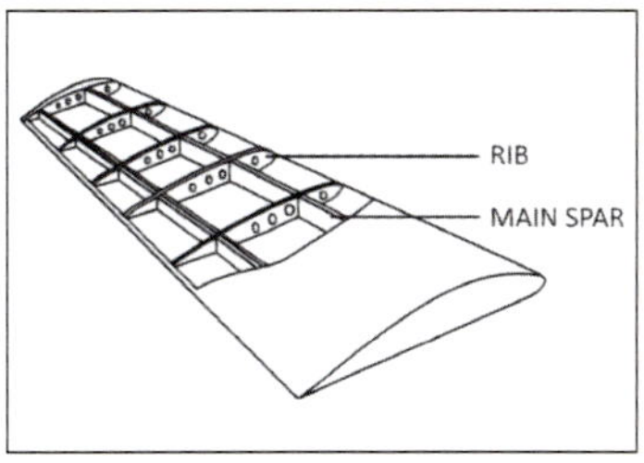

15. ANSWER C

FURTHER READING: APM VOLUME 4, SECTION 2, CHAPTER 15 – THE AIRFRAME

16. (Answer: A) Flying control locks are used on the ground to ensure that the control surfaces are not damaged in high winds.

FURTHER READING: APM VOLUME 4, SECTION 2, CHAPTER 15 – THE AIRFRAME

17. (Answer: C) Wing spars carry the major loads experienced by the wing. Upward bending loads are experienced where lift is generated to support the aircraft in flight. These forces are often offset by carrying fuel in the wings or employing wing-tip mounted fuel tanks. Downward bending loads are experienced whilst stationary on the ground due to the weight of the structure, fuel carried in the wings, and possibly wing-mounted engines.

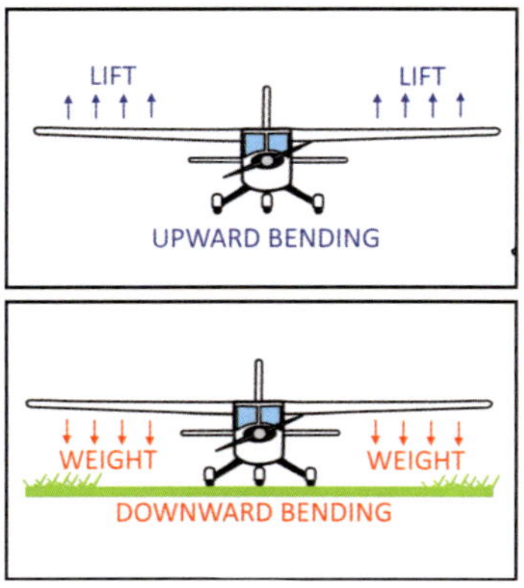

17. ANSWER C

FURTHER READING: APM VOLUME 4, SECTION 4, CHAPTER 29 – AIRFRAME LIMITATIONS

18. (Answer: B) A pilot can identify tyre creep using the two alignment, or "creep" marks, one of which is painted on the tyre side wall and one on the wheel flange. The marks need to be aligned for the tyre to be considered serviceable, if they have moved more than the width of the mark attention is necessary.

18. ANSWER B

FURTHER READING: APM VOLUME 4, SECTION 2, CHAPTER 24 – LANDING GEAR, TYRES AND BRAKES

19. (Answer: C) With regard to a magnetic compass, the correct statements are 2, 3 and 4.

1. A magnetic compass does not suffer from turning or acceleration errors

2. The fluid within the compass supports the weight of the magnet, decreases friction and dampens oscillations

3. The aeroplane moves around the compass magnet

4. When deviation is applied to the compass heading we get the magnetic heading

5. When variation is applied to the compass heading we get the magnetic heading

1. The compass suffers from both turning and acceleration errors as a result of magnetic dip leading to the weight of the magnet not being directly underneath the pivot. Magnetic dip is due to the magnet trying to align itself with the earth's magnetic field which is practically horizontal at the equator, but almost vertical at the poles. Arranging the magnet as a pendulum does alleviate some of the problem, but will not eradicate it totally.

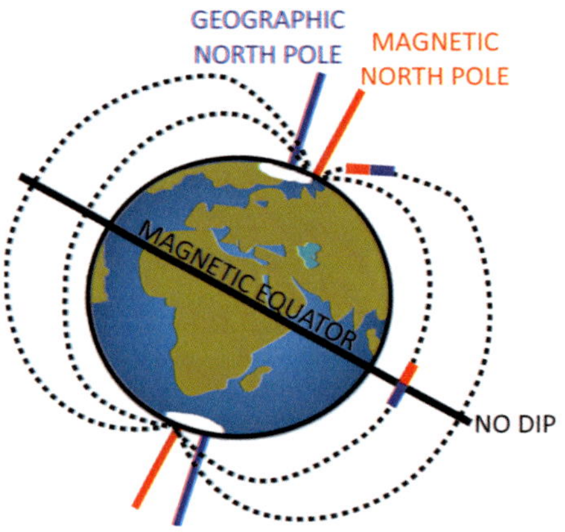

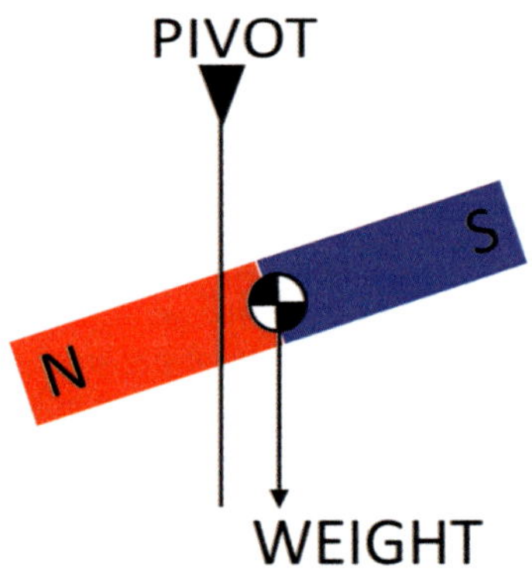

ACCELERATION ERRORS

As the aircraft changes speed the compass magnet is left behind due to inertia. As the magnet's weight is not directly under the pivot, this lag will mean the compass will swing away from the correct magnetic direction. Acceleration errors are most pronounced on easterly or westerly headings.

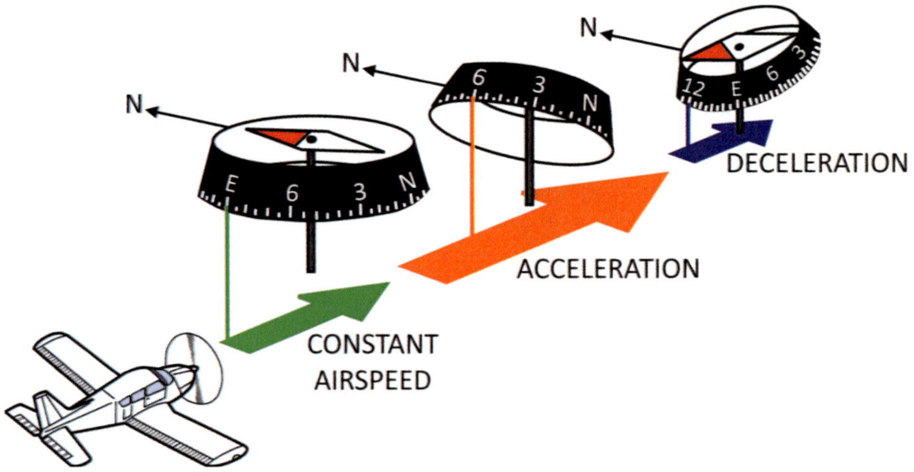

Heading	Acceleration	Deceleration
Easterly	Apparent turn north	Apparent turn south
Westerly	Apparent turn north	Apparent turn south
ANDS: Acceleration gives an apparent turn North; Deceleration gives an apparent turn South.		

COMPASS ACCELERATION ERRORS

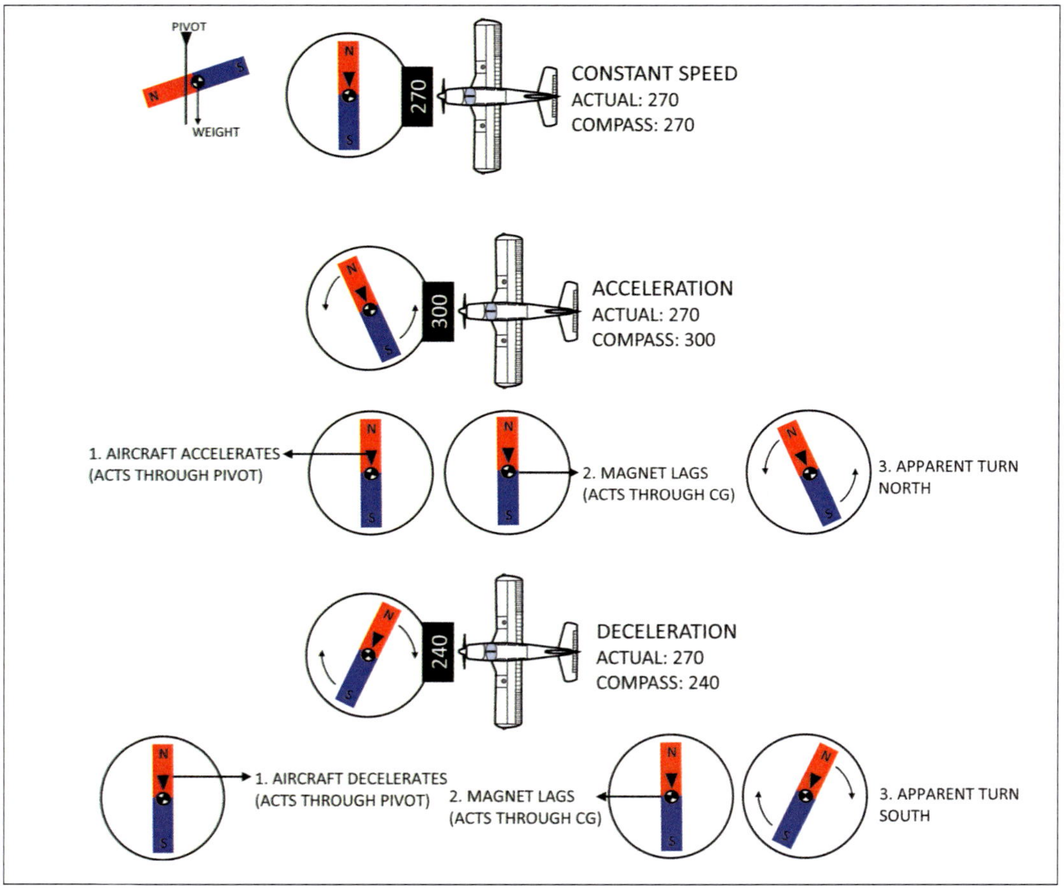

COMPASS TURNING ERRORS

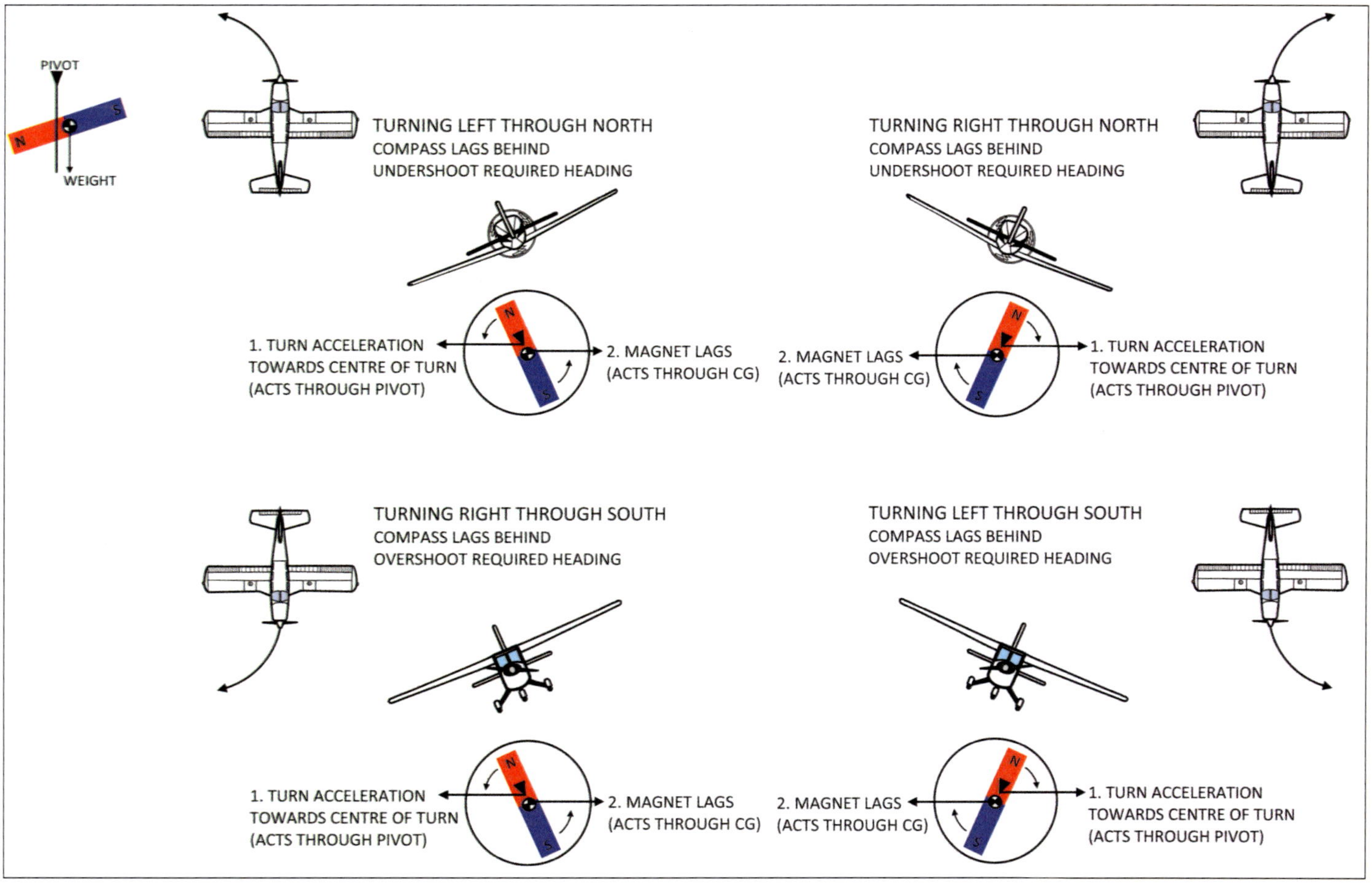

TURNING ERRORS

Turning errors are derived from centripetal force acting towards the centre of the turn. Again the magnet's inertia causes it to lag behind the actual aircraft. This time the errors are at their greatest when turning through north or south. See diagrams on previous page.

2. The fluid within the compass supports the weight of the magnet, decreases friction and dampens oscillations. This is true. The liquid should be observed before flight to ensure that it is free of bubbles and not discoloured.

3. The aeroplane moves around the compass magnet. Again, this option is correct.

4. When deviation is applied to the compass heading we get the magnetic heading. The magnetic compass will not only sense the earth's magnetic field, but also any other field nearby. In an aircraft magnetic fields may be generated by rotating parts of the engine, radio installations and other electronic devices. The combined effect of these magnetic fields is called deviation; it is a measure of how much the compass is made to deviate from magnetic north. Each aircraft will have a deviation card which will show the correction that needs to be applied to a compass reading to obtain the magnetic heading.

TRUE variation MAGNETIC deviation COMPASS
T v M d C

5. Variation is the angular difference between true north and magnetic north. It is applied to the true heading to obtain the magnetic heading.

FURTHER READING: APM VOLUME 4, SECTION 3, CHAPTER 27 – THE MAGNETIC COMPASS

20. **(Answer: C)** During a pre-flight inspection of the brakes it is important to check that the brake discs are not corroded. Additionally the discs should not be pitted. Other items to inspect are that the assembly is firmly attached and that there are no leaks of hydraulic fluid from the brake lines.

FURTHER READING: APM VOLUME 4, SECTION 2, CHAPTER 24 – LANDING GEAR, TYRES AND BRAKES

END OF EXPLANATIONS PAPER 4

INTENTIONALLY BLANK

ANSWER SHEETS

NOTE: *Please feel free to photocopying these answer sheet pages when practising tests. All other pages are subject to the copyright law and should not be copied under any circumstances.*

PAPER NO.				
	A	B	C	D
1				
2				
3				
4				
5				
6				
7				
8				
9				
10				
11				
12				
13				
14				
15				
16				
17				
18				
19				

PAPER NO.				
	A	B	C	D
1				
2				
3				
4				
5				
6				
7				
8				
9				
10				
11				
12				
13				
14				
15				
16				
17				
18				
19				
20				

PAPER NO.				
	A	B	C	D
1				
2				
3				
4				
5				
6				
7				
8				
9				
10				
11				
12				
13				
14				
15				
16				
17				
18				
19				
20				

PAPER NO.				
	A	B	C	D
1				
2				
3				
4				
5				
6				
7				
8				
9				
10				
11				
12				
13				
14				
15				
16				
17				
18				
19				
20				

PAPER NO.				
	A	B	C	D
1				
2				
3				
4				
5				
6				
7				
8				
9				
10				
11				
12				
13				
14				
15				
16				
17				
18				
19				
20				

PAPER NO.				
	A	B	C	D
1				
2				
3				
4				
5				
6				
7				
8				
9				
10				
11				
12				
13				
14				
15				
16				
17				
18				
19				
20				

PAPER NO.				
	A	B	C	D
1				
2				
3				
4				
5				
6				
7				
8				
9				
10				
11				
12				
13				
14				
15				
16				
17				
18				
19				
20				

PAPER NO.				
	A	B	C	D
1				
2				
3				
4				
5				
6				
7				
8				
9				
10				
11				
12				
13				
14				
15				
16				
17				
18				
19				
20				

PAPER NO.				
	A	B	C	D
1				
2				
3				
4				
5				
6				
7				
8				
9				
10				
11				
12				
13				
14				
15				
16				
17				
18				
19				
20				

PAPER NO.				
	A	B	C	D
1				
2				
3				
4				
5				
6				
7				
8				
9				
10				
11				
12				
13				
14				
15				
16				
17				
18				
19				
20				

PAPER NO.				
	A	B	C	D
1				
2				
3				
4				
5				
6				
7				
8				
9				
10				
11				
12				
13				
14				
15				
16				
17				
18				
19				
20				

PAPER NO.				
	A	B	C	D
1				
2				
3				
4				
5				
6				
7				
8				
9				
10				
11				
12				
13				
14				
15				
16				
17				
18				
19				
20				